# British Perspectives on Terrorism

*Edited by*

## Paul Wilkinson

*Professor of International Relations,
University of Aberdeen*

London
GEORGE ALLEN & UNWIN
Boston          Sydney

© 1981, Crane, Russak & Company, Inc.

**George Allen & Unwin (Publishers) Ltd,**
**40 Museum Street, London WC1A 1LU, UK**

George Allen & Unwin (Publishers) Ltd,
Park Lane, Hemel Hempstead, Herts HP2 4TE, UK

Allen & Unwin Inc.,
9 Winchester Terrace, Winchester, Mass 01890, USA

George Allen & Unwin Australia Pty Ltd,
8 Napier Street, North Sydney, NSW 2060, Australia

First published in 1981
as Volume 5, Nos. 1 & 2 *Terrorism: An International Journal*

---

**British Library Cataloguing in Publication Data**

British perspectives on terrorism.
1. Terrorism – Addresses, essays, lectures.
I. Wilkinson, Paul
322.4'2     HV6431


ISBN 0–04–327064–6
ISBN 0–04–327065–4 Pbk

---

**Library of Congress Cataloging in Publication Data**

Main entry under title:
British perspectives on terrorism.
    "First published in 1981 as volume 5, nos. 1 & 2, Terrorism: an international journal" – T.p. verso.
    Contents: Introduction/Paul Wilkinson – Politics and propaganda of the Provisional IRA/Maurice Tugwell – The water and the fish/E. Moxon-Browne – [etc.]
    1. Terrorism – Great Britain – Addresses, essays, lectures.
2. Terrorism – Northern Ireland – Addresses, essays, lectures.
3. Terrorism – Addresses, essays, lectures.  I. Wilkinson, Paul.
II. Terrorism; v. 5, no. 1–2.
HV6433.G7B74     303.6'2     81–7937


ISBN 0–04–327064–6          AACR2
ISBN 0–04–327065–4 (pbk.)

---

Printed in Great Britain by Biddles Ltd, Guildford, Surrey

# Contents

# Introduction

## Paul Wilkinson

The strengths and weaknesses of British research and writing on terrorism reflect, to an almost uncanny extent, the basic paradox of the recent British experience of political violence. The fact is that Great Britain has enjoyed freedom from major internal strife and violence for over one hundred and fifty years: the last mainland armed rebellion against the Crown was in 1745 and England, Scotland, and Wales have been virtually free of mass riots and disorders since the early nineteenth century. Yet, in total contrast, "John Bull's other Island" experienced a whole series of bloody internal conflicts throughout this period, from the Wolf Tone Rebellion to the Irish independence struggle of 1919–21, and the grim civil war that followed.

Thus, for successive British governments in the nineteenth and early twentieth centuries, serious internal violence was essentially a *colonial* problem, an inescapable element of the White Man's Burden which only reached British popular awareness as a series of battle honors won by the small all-volunteer British Army in defense of the Empire. Hence, from the British perspective, terrorism, violent insurrection, and guerrilla warfare were phenomena experienced by unfortunate and unruly foreigners. Almost by definition, such things did not, indeed *could not,* occur in the mother country where, according to fashionable belief, progress had wrought a parliamentary democracy and a rule of law in which such reversions to tooth and claw were not merely unlikely but unthinkable.

This enormous psychological gulf between domestic tranquility and foreign strife continued, indeed was strengthened, in the post-1945 period. For despite the almost continuous efforts by British governments of the 1950s and 1960s to negotiate peaceful handovers to independence movements in former colonies in Asia, Africa, and the Middle East, violence did occur, prior to independence being negotiated, in Malaya, Kenya, Cyprus, Aden, and Rhodesia, and prior to the relinquishing of the British mandate in Palestine. Critics and detractors of British policy in these areas often claim that these conflicts were entirely the fault of British administrations. No doubt there were numerous errors of judgment in the making and execution of policy. But it should be remembered that the British authorities had inherited particularly intractable political problems in all these areas.

In Palestine, Cyprus, Aden, and Rhodesia the efforts to achieve a peaceful transition were bedeviled by civil war between rival ethnic and political groups battling to take control within each country. Thus, in these cases, the British government was unable to deal with any single bargaining agent in the colony that enjoyed support and legitimacy in the eyes of the whole population. And in all these cases, with the exception of Rhodesia, British forces became sucked into the internecine conflict in an effort to restore order and stability.

By the time of Mr. Ian Smith's 1965 Unilateral Declaration of Independence in Rhodesia Britain was too weakened, militarily and economically, to intervene to restore Crown authority. Mr. Harold Wilson, British Prime Minister at that time, and his colleagues, possessed neither the will nor the means to act.

Terrorism played a considerable part in these postwar conflicts: in Palestine, Cyprus, and Aden it is fair to say that it played the major role in bringing about what has been called "the assets-to-liabilities shift" in British perceptions of long-term interests in maintaining a presence in these countries. In other words, groups such as the Stern Gang, EOKA, and FLOSY were largely successful in using the weapon of coercive intimidation—murders and threats of murders—against British troops, police, and civilians. War weary and increasingly impoverished, British governments, backed by public opinion, were pushed to the point at which they preferred British withdrawal to the sacrifice of more and more British lives.

There are a number of important points to be made about this experience of the terrorist weapon in the colonial setting. Firstly, Britain's experiences were by no means unique. Other European colonial powers, and in particular France, also encountered this form of violence on a large scale. Indeed in its conflict with the FLN in Algeria, the French authorities and troops and the Algerian civil population suffered a far more savage war of this nature than anything Britain confronted in the decolonizing period. Second, the British authorities quite early on in this postwar period, became depressingly familiar not only with the tragic cost in lives levied against their own troops and other personnel but also with the widespread use of repressive terror by rebel groups against their own people, in order to "neutralize" them or to coerce them into denying cooperation to the colonial authorities, and to force them to supply or otherwise actively assist the rebels. It is worth recalling that far more Africans than Europeans died at the hands of the Mau Mau in Kenya. The same is true of the conflicts in Malaya and Aden, and, later, in the Rhodesian civil war.

A third important consequence was that it was the British Army that continued to be charged with the main responsibility for restoring and maintaining order in these bitter conflicts. Inevitably therefore they developed a huge reservoir of practical knowledge, expertise, strategy, and tactics, covering not only guerrilla warfare generally but also the rapidly proliferating challenge from urban terrorism. Hence, just as some of the finest early analyses of guerrilla warfare were produced by soldiers or temporary soldiers (one thinks of such books as C. E. Callwell's *Small Wars, Their Principles and Practice*, 1899, and T. E. Lawrence's *Revolt in the Desert*, 1927), some of the best recent British writing on terrorism has been by soldiers or ex-soldiers who acquired their practical knowledge and experience of the subject in the unconventional wars of the 1950s and 1960s.[1]

A fourth consequence of this long experience of terrorism in the context of colonial conflict is significant in a very different way. The apparent successes of groups such as EOKA in using the weapon of terrorism against Britain undoubtedly stimulated others to emulate them. This model of what may be termed "anti-colonial terrorism" still plays an important part in shaping the strategy and propaganda of groups such as the Provisional IRA, for example, even though the real conflict situation in Northern Ireland is so vastly different in many respects. It is worth noting that—whether by tragic coincidence or sheer irresponsible folly—the IRA men imprisoned for raiding an armory in England in 1953 were placed in the company of jailed EOKA terrorists![2]

By the mid-1960s informed opinion in Britain generally assumed that once the turmoil of the colonial independence struggles was over the home country could return to cultivating its own somewhat neglected economic garden in domestic peace and tranquility. It was, of course, the birth of a renewed and bloody conflict in Ireland, periodically spilling over into Provisional IRA attacks on the British mainland, that shattered these hopes. Britain, at least so far, has been fortunate in remaining largely free of indigenous neo-Marxist and nihilist terrorism. In the early 1970s there was a small and amateurish campaign by a group calling itself the Angry Brigade, which carried out a bomb attack on the home of the then Home Secretary, Mr. Robert Carr.[3] But there has been no British parallel to the Red Army Faction, the Red Brigades, the Japanese United Red Army, or even the American Weathermen. This is just as well, for the British government, army, and police have had their hands full in coping with the terrorism emanating from Northern Ireland with all its tragic consequences for the life of that unhappy province of the United Kingdom.

It is difficult for those who have not witnessed conditions in Northern Ireland, particularly in West Belfast, and the border areas of South Armagh, Fermanagh, and Tyrone, to understand the severity and intractability of the Northern Ireland conflict.[4] Over 2,000 lives have been lost in the decade of violence since 1970, and thousands more have been injured. American readers will get a better idea of the magnitude of this violence if they translate it into equivalent proportions of their own population. The U.S. population being 138 times that of Northern Ireland, the province's total casualty figures would mean, in American terms, a staggering 276,000 deaths and over 1½ million injured. Can one seriously doubt that if the United States had experienced such casualties the conflict would have been regarded as a major internal war, and its peaceful resolution given the highest priority? Over £200 million has been paid out in compensation for damage to property in the province since 1969. Whole areas of Belfast look as though they have been subjected to repeated aerial bombardment. Industry has been starved of investment in what was already an economically depressed region of the United Kingdom. And a whole generation has grown up in the province under the shadow of the gunman and the bomber, constantly aware of the threat of a fresh eruption of violence.

The Northern Ireland conflict since 1969 has produced the worst protracted campaign of terrorism experienced in Western Europe in recent history. Almost from the outset the British Army had to be brought in to take responsibility for protecting the Catholic minority population and keeping the peace. Mr. James Callaghan, the Home Secretary in the Labor government of the day (1970), had no other choice but to call in the Army to aid the civil power, because, under the strain of the disorders, the police service (the Royal Ulster Constabulary) and the B "Specials," so feared and hated by the minority, were clearly unable to maintain law and order.[5] It is true that the British Army had long experience of counterinsurgency and peacekeeping in the vastly different contexts of colonial conflicts to draw upon. But this is certainly not why they were first introduced in Northern Ireland. All concerned with the decision to deploy troops in the province and the commanders responsible for carrying out their remit were aware that the circumstances of their new task were quite exceptional and difficult. Troops had not been used on such a large scale for internal peacekeeping within the United Kingdom for over a century. Nor had they ever before had to perform such a politically delicate task under all the constitutional and judicial restraints of parliamentary democracy, among their own fellow citizens, and under the full glare of television and the press. They have had to operate at the most dangerous mid-levels of coerciveness, walking a tightrope between over- and under-reaction, constantly aware of the need for impartiality in the upholding of the law as between the Protestant majority and the Catholic minority. The Army has acquired a sophisticated and probably unrivaled expertise in coping with the problems of terrorism in a Western democratic society.

Since 1976 the British government has used its opportunities under direct rule, and its emergency powers, to curb the terrorist violence of both the Provisional IRA and the extremist Protestant groups. They have also been highly successful in rebuilding the Royal Ulster Constabulary and establishing police primacy in the maintenance of the rule of law in the province. This has involved establishing the police reputation for impartiality as between the majority and minority communities, and reinstituting a police presence and regular patrols in areas where, a few years ago, this would have seemed impossible. The Army, which has played such a vital role in achieving the security conditions required for the switch to police primacy, is, of course, still indispensable. In the troubled border areas, the so-called "bandit-country," the Army is literally the only force capable of upholding law and order.

While lives are still being lost through terrorism, and while deep and bitter political differences over the future governance of the province prevail, it would be premature to assume that a peaceful resolution is even in sight. Nevertheless, the continuing gradual improvement in the security situation, the decline in the numbers of civilian casualties, and the apparent determination of the British Cabinet and the new Secretary of State for Northern Ireland to impose a political framework on the province which is manifestly fair to both minority and majority populations, give grounds for hope. It may well be the case that, in a province so blitzed and politically and economically damaged by prolonged violence, the local politicians are simply morally and intellectually incapable of arriving at such a framework unaided. And it should be remembered that it is the British government and people *as a whole* that have borne the major burden, both militarily and economically, for propping up the ailing province. The soldiers who have given their lives in the fight against terrorism have come from every corner of the United Kingdom. It is Western and British defenses *as a whole* that have suffered from the constant diversion of Army manpower away from its designated NATO role and into the frustrating and heartbreaking tasks of peacekeeping in Northern Ireland. It is the British taxpayers who in 1979 alone paid out £860 million to subsidize the struggling Northern Ireland economy. Hence the present British government, with its secure parliamentary majority and three-quarters of its term still ahead of it, has an unrivaled opportunity to exert leadership over Northern Ireland. If necessary, it must impose a solution acceptable in the eyes of the United Kingdom parliament, one which can command at least a minimal requisite degree of acceptance and support from *both* majority *and* minority populations in Northern Ireland. In the meantime, if this political progress is to have any chance of success, the security war to curb and suppress terrorism must be pursued with the greatest possible professionalism, political sensitivity, determination, and vigor.

National interest may not be the most noble rationale for policy. One would perhaps like to think that the British government would want to provide international leadership in increasing and inproving cooperation against terrorism because terrorist atrocities are an unmitigated evil wherever they occur, and because the rights of the innocent and the rule of law ought to be protected throughout the international community. Nor should we forget our moral obligations to that smaller group of states, our Western friends and allies of NATO. If the North Atlantic community of states is to have any true meaning, value, and solidarity, the conduct of relations between the Western allies must be based, at the very least, on the precept ''Do as you would be done by.'' We owe it to each other to render all possible moral and practical support against the dangerous menace of terrorists who increasingly conduct their operations transnationally. And in these times, when the political and economic health and cohesiveness of the Alliance is so vital to all the Western states' security, we should realize that a campaign of violence aimed at destabilizing any one of our members is a threat to all.

It would be unduly pessimistic to assume that Britain is any less responsive than others to these wider claims of international obligation. Indeed, if one examines the recent experience of international response against terrorism, one finds that a few British voices have played a leading part in demanding an uncompromising international stand against terrorism as part of a general effort to uphold the basic principles of international law and morality. A much larger group, including leading politicians of British's three main political parties, is prepared to accept that we must act as ''good neighbors'' within the North Atlantic alliance and the European Community by helping to foster cooperation in combatting terrorism, at least within the frontiers of the Alliance.

Even if this were not the case, it should be obvious that Britain has the strongest *national interest* in formulating an effective policy to counter domestic and international terrorism. We have a vital interest in ending the terrorist campaign in Northern Ireland, a campaign that has been a running sore in the United Kingdom's body politic for over a decade. Britain has a vital concern in curbing the spillover of international terrorism from the Middle East, Europe, and elsewhere into our large international diplomatic and business community in London. Thirdly, the British government has a major responsibility to help safeguard the lives of British diplomats, business executives and other private citizens, and British property and interests against the rapidly escalating international terrorist attacks mounted against them abroad. The plight of the American diplomats held hostage in Iran may have misled Europeans into assuming that they are exempt from major acts of international terrorism. There are no grounds whatever for such complacency. It is obvious that American life and property will continue to remain a major terrorist target in the foreseeable future. But it should be equally clear that the West European allies are among the most likely targets to be hit in the sudden explosions of anti-Western fury and hate that occur in the Third World.[6] Britain and France, in particular, have been reviled as imperialist powers, allegedly guilty of untold exploitation and injustices in the past, and are now charged with crimes of neocolonialism. British embassies have been sacked and seized by mobs. Some of our diplomats, businessmen, and other citizens abroad have been taken hostage. Some have been murdered or seriously injured in terrorist attacks. It should not be forgotten, for example, that British diplomats were among those who suffered in the first great wave of diplomatic kidnappings in 1970–1971. Mr. James Cross was kidnapped by FLQ terrorists in Québec in October 1970. And Sir Geoffrey Jackson suffered nine months of incarceration by the Tupamaros in 1971. Sir Geoffrey wrote an account of his experiences in *People's Prison*,[7] a classic of the literature on terrorism.

Britain shares the West's strategic interest in preserving stability in sensitive and vital regions, such as the southern flank of NATO and the Persian Gulf. Because domestic or foreign-inspired terrorism may help to subvert our allies and friends in these areas, Britain has a direct interest in assisting and strengthening her allies' internal defenses. Nor should we overlook the possibility that terrorist attacks may be used to provoke international crises and wider conflagrations, or that it can be employed by the Soviets and their proxies to direct attention from yet another swift intervention on the model of Afghanistan, or to "soften up" our potential for resistance at the inception of a major military assault on NATO Europe.

It is fortunate that Britain has been able to develop special strengths and resources to deal with the challenges of modern terrorism. The leaderships of both major parties have learned valuable lessons from their periods in office, both from the handling of the security situation in Northern Ireland and from dealing with a whole range of terrorist incidents at home and abroad, from kidnappings and barricade-and-hostage situations to assassinations. Both Mr. William Whitelaw, the present Home Secretary, and Mr. Merlyn Rees, Shadow Home Secretary, formerly held the post of Secretary of State for Northern Ireland. Their great personal experience and their expertise in this field have provided an invaluable continuity at governmental level. There is, to all intents and purposes, a bipartisan approach to antiterrorist policy and legislation. Mr. Merlyn Rees has contributed a valuable essay to this issue of the journal which draws on this experience, dealing with British legislation on the prevention of terrorism.

The two most important practical resources Britain has developed to tackle terrorism are its antiterrorist police and the Special Air Service (SAS) Regiment which is specially trained for hostage rescue. Police successes include the handling of the Spaghetti House and Balcombe Street sieges and the recent siege at the Iranian Embassy at Princes Gate. SAS successes include the support they gave to the GSG-9 commando operation to rescue hostages from a Lufthansa plane hijacked to Mogadishu in 1977, and their spectacular success in rescuing hostages in the Iranian Embassy siege of May 1980.[8] Tony Geraghty, defense correspondent of the London *Sunday Times*, has just published an authoritative historical portrait of the SAS—a remarkable achievement in view of the regiment's legendary secrecy and its dislike of any publicity for individual members.

In a special article for this British issue of *Terrorism*, Dr. Frank Gregory of Southampton University gives a concise assessment of the way the British police have adapted their organization, methods, and training to deal with the challenge of terrorism. Those in other countries who admire the streamlined coordination and professionalism of the British police response to this problem will read Dr. Gregory's analysis with great interest, for he approaches his subject with critical perception, bringing out some of the practical problems and difficulties the police have encountered. In my own view the real secret of the success of the British police in the antiterrorism role is the extremely high standard of specialist training afforded, both at command level and to the specialist officers of the elite antiterrorist squad. As one who has been involved in this training for some years I can testify to the considerable efforts made to keep the training balanced as between theory and practice, comprehensive, and thoroughly up-to-date.

No special issue on British perspectives on terrorism worthy of the name could avoid giving prominence to the bloody and long-drawn-out Northern Ireland conflict. Our four opening articles are a major contribution to our understanding of the origins, aims, and tactics of the Provisional IRA, the social and political implications of the violence, and the response of the British authorities and public.

Jillian Becker is a self-exiled South African novelist who wrote a brilliant study of the Baader-Meinhof Gang. *Hitler's Children* has been justly praised as an outstanding study of the group psychology and individual mentality of members of a terrorist gang. We are proud to include her work in this representative selection on British perspectives on terrorism. She is a brilliantly percipient student of the subject, and as a South African liberal writer she has chosen to leave the country of her birth and live and work in London. She maintains her interest in the study of violence and extremism, and has contributed to major international conferences on aspects of the subject. Jillian Becker's fascinating exploration of the mental world and belief systems of terrorists provokes the thought that insufficient attention has been given to the reeducation and rehabilitation of those "supporters" who have fallen victim to one or other of the fanatical cults of modern terrorism. Yet this would be the most effective form of social prophylaxis of all. If we could prevent or at least radically reduce the flow of young recruits into terrorist organizations by effectively countering the spiritual and moral corruption of tiny subcultures that nurture philosophies of violence and hatred, terrorism in our Western democracies would ultimately wither away.

The concluding articles are representative of the growing body of work by British academics on problems of international terrorism and international response. Dr. Richard Clutterbuck, who assesses the development of British kidnap risk management, has been a major pioneer in specialist research into political violence, and he has an intimate knowledge of kidnap and ransom insurance and security consultancy. His general study of the subject, *Kidnap and Ransom* (London: Faber, 1978), should be compulsory reading for all diplomatists and business executives posted to high-risk zones. This study is usefully complemented by Caroline Moorehead's *Fortune's Hostages* (London: Hamish Hamilton, 1980), which contains much erudition and insight on the history of kidnapping and the relationship between the kidnappers and their anguished victims.

In a concluding piece I have attempted a concise summary of proposals for government and international responses to terrorism appropriate for liberal democracies. They are controversial but their objective is improved international protection of the innocent.

## Notes

1. See notably Major-General Frank Kitson, *Low Intensity Operations* (London: Faber, 1971) and *Bunch of Five* (London: Faber, 1978), and Major-General Richard Clutterbuck, *Living with Terrorism* (London: Faber, 1975) and *Kidnap and Ransom* (London: Faber, 1978).

2. Sean MacStioFain, *Memoirs of a Revolutionary* (London: Gordon Cremonesi, 1975), pp. 74–79.

3. For an interesting account, see Gordon Carr, *The Angry Brigade* (London: Gollancz, 1975).

4. On the background and development of the conflict, see: Owen Dudley Edwards, *The Sins of Our Fathers: Roots of Conflict in Northern Ireland* (Dublin, 1970); Conor Cruise O'Brien, *States of Ireland* (New York, 1972); Liam de Paor, *Divided Ulster* (Harmondsworth, 1970); Sunday Times Insight Team, *Ulster* (Harmondsworth, 1972); Robert Kee, *The Green Flag, A History of Irish Nationalism* (London, 1974); Richard Rose, *Governing without Consensus* (Boston, 1971); J. Bowyer Bell, *The Secret Army: The IRA 1916–1979* (Dublin, 1979); and Peter Janke, *Ulster: A Decade of Violence* (London: Institute for the Study of Conflict, 1979).

5. Mr. James Callaghan gives a useful account of the constraints operating on the British government when this decision was made in his book *A House Divided* (1972).

6. For an assessment of current threats and trends in terrorist tactics and targets, see Paul Wilkinson, *Terrorism: International Dimensions—Answering the Challenge* (London: Institute for the Study of Conflict, 1979).

7. Published in the United States under the title *Surviving the Long Night* (New York: Vanguard, 1974).

8. Sir Robert Mark, Metropolitan Police Commissioner at the time of these

sieges, gives an interesting personal account of the lessons learned by the British police in *The Office of Constable* (1978). But for the contrary view, see George Brock, Robin Lustig, Laurence Marks et al., *Siege: Six Days at the Iranian Embassy* (London: Macmillan, 1980).

# Politics and Propaganda of the Provisional IRA

Maurice Tugwell

University of New Brunswick

*Abstract*        So long as the declared objective of the Provisional IRA's violent campaign was the abolition of the Protestant-dominated Northern Ireland Government, many Northern Catholics gave political or moral support. Propaganda mobilized this audience and was also directed outwards, mainly towards America and Britain, utilizing ancient myths, current allegations or revolutionary fervor according to the taste of each audience. But once Stormont had fallen, the Provisionals were unable to convince their supporters that the IRA had been wise to reject negotiations offered by the UK Government and instead to adhere to a strategy of uniting Ireland by force. Violence became an end in itself, appealing only to minority audiences held under propaganda's spell, and diminishing rather than enhancing the prospects of a united Ireland.

"The Provisionals in effect left the official IRA, not so much because of a fundamental disagreement over long-term ideological issues, but because certain strong-minded personalities wanted to engage in full-scale guerrilla warfare immediately, and formed their own group to do so. The niceties of political debate they left, and still leave, to the future."—*Peter J. Villiers*[1]

"The moral right to wage war of liberation has never been questioned: the moral right, in fact duty, of challenging a foreign oppressive army of occupation, in our case that of a one-time colonial power, Great Britain, *has never been questioned in the long and bitter history of Ireland.*" —*P. Ó' Néill*[2]

These two quotations contain most of the essential truths of Provisional IRA motivation. Irish resistance to British rule has traditionally followed two roads, the constitutional and the violent, and has been at its most effective when the two have worked together. The myths that have arisen out of twentieth-century resistance have, however, tended to dwell entirely on the violence, glorifying not just the end, but the means, and promoting the theory that physical force alone can solve political problems.[3] The men who formed the Provisional IRA in 1969—John Stephenson, Rory O'Brady, Leo Martin, Billy McKee, Francis Card, and Seamus Twomey—were steeped in this mythology. Their primary enemy was Britain, seen as the occupying power in the six northern countries of an Ireland whose assumed right to unity is written into its Republican constitution.[4] Their chief political aim was and still is to achieve this unity, within a socialist, federalist Ireland.[5]

Political violence, like war, is a continuation of politics by other means. To be rational, political violence must therefore pursue realistic, achievable goals. This article will argue that from the formation of the Provisional Wing of the IRA in 1969 until the proroguing of the Northern Ireland government in March 1972, political violence was effective as part of an ad hoc alignment of social, political, and paramilitary forces, but that since that date the Provisional campaign has been counterproductive to the movement's ambitions. We will examine the relationships between politics and propaganda, and propaganda and violence, and assess Provisional strengths and weaknesses in these areas.

## The Situation in 1969

When in 1969 the Provisionals began what was intended to be a war of national liberation against the British presence in Northern Ireland, they had three sociological trends working strongly in their favor—the British acquired habit of withdrawal in the face of violence, the example of Vietnam, and the civil rights movement. Britain had just quit one of her last remaining colonies, Aden, after a total breakdown of law and order achieved by terroristic violence. The outgoing government even allowed power to pass into the hands of a Moscow-backed Marxist faction, so that within a short period of time Aden's naval and air facilities were under Soviet control.[6] Britain's orderly withdrawal from empire had in this instance become a political rout, while the pattern of response to revolutionary violence in overseas territories seemed almost invariable—shrill denials that the government would ever yield to force; more violence, pack up and go home. After 24 years of such with-drawals, the British public seemed well conditioned to this pattern, which appeared to offer the least painful escape from what many accepted as a necessary historical process.

This was also one year after the Tet offensive in Vietnam, when the United States news media turned what had in fact been a considerable military success for the South into a massive political and psychological victory for the North, one that was ultimately to contaminate the whole campaign.[7] The power of the media to influence public perceptions of conflict situations and to undermine political will was established, to the satisfaction of radicals and many liberals, and to the chagrin of estab-lished power and those responsible for countering violence. The rev-olutionary basked in the warmth of public admiration, while the police and the military tended to be portrayed as misguided or willful oppres-sors. This indulgence of what Bernard Levin calls "fun revolution" had been reinforced by civil rights movements, which had brought masses of fair-minded citizens into confrontation with law enforcement agents. The line between righteous protest and insurrectionary violence was often hard to define and, when in doubt, media and public sympathy generally reached out to the apparent underdog.

The Provisionals sought to make use of all these positive factors. Seeing Northern Ireland merely as another British colony awaiting liberation, their leaders calculated that the killing of British soldiers would soon influence government policy. Maria McGuire, a senior defector from the movement, has described how the I.R.A.'s "Army Council" agreed to kill 36 British soldiers—the same number that had died in Aden—but later raised this figure to 80.[8] This, they believed, would force the British to negotiate a withdrawal. Like Pearse and Connolly 53 years earlier,[9] the Provisionals preferred to ignore the one million Protestant Irish who composed the "loyal" Northern majority, and instead believed their own propaganda theme which depicted Northern Ireland as a captive province, held in unwilling thrall by Britain. Armed with native wit and inspired by the brilliant propagan-dists of the 1919–21 guerrilla war,[10] the Provisional leaders were quick to appreciate the importance of friendly or ambivalent journalists, and sought from an early date to have the Ulster conflict reported as "Britain's Vietnam.'"[11] Links to the news media were cemented at the outset by Provisional infiltration of the Northern Ireland Civil Rights Association (NICRA), whose endeavors to expose and end Protestant majority discrimination against Northern Catholics earned that movement well deserved sympathy and support.

In contrast to these positive assets, the Provisionals had to contend, initially, with two severe handicaps. British troops, who had been deployed in a police role in Northern Ireland in 1969, had provided protection for hard-pressed Northern Catholics against sectarian attacks and the allegedly partial and rough attentions of the Royal Ulster Constabulary (RUC). Catholics were therefore well disposed toward these soldiers.[12] Moreover these Catholics, in spite of unity being a cherished, distant ideal, had little enthusiasm for a war of liberation against the British: their grievances and fears were directed against the apparatus of Protestant political and economic domination in the North, symbolized and to a large extent exercised in the Northern Ireland parliament and government at Stormont, outside Belfast. The Provisionals knew that the first handicap could and must be overcome. The second was evidently accepted as being beyond their powers to alter, at least at this early stage. They therefore decided to sharpen and direct the existing sentiment, using it as a tactical mean toward their strategic goal. They would mobilize the Catholic masses around the banner "Smash Stormont," and in the process they could consign the British soldiers to the role of "traditional enemy," while they assumed the defense of Catholic areas. "Smash Stormont" appealed to both NICRA and its supporters, and to various Catholic political parties in Northern Ireland. "People's Democracy," a left-leaning, mainly student group was eager to respond, and the Social Democratic and Labor Party (SDLP) was persuaded (some say, at the point of the gun) to boycott the parliament and join the campaign. The SDLP contained many of the brightest political figures in Catholic Ulster and, in so far as the party's policies overlapped those of the Provisionals, their spokesmen acted as credible and persuasive agents of anti-Stormont propaganda. Almost by chance the Provisionals created the kind of joint constitutional-military alliance that had been effective in Ireland's past. Militant leaders were freed of the need to explain policy, as the tactical objective had already attracted widespread support and was skillfully articulated by the SDLP and others. Instead, they could concentrate on violence and on propaganda, which in this campaign were pretty much the same thing.

## Theory of the "Asset-to-Liability Shift"

In some revolutions, success is achieved by the physical conquest of the government forces. There may be a long buildup while the rebels progress through a survival phase, protracted war, and then mobile warfare, but in the end of the insurgent forces win a decisive victory in open battle. In many revolutionary situations, however, this procedure is impossible. There is no prospect that rebel military strength will ever match that of the government. Victory, if it is to be won at all, must come about by indirect means. Government forces have to be out-flanked, and this has to be accomplished by a psychological attack which causes the government to abandon the struggle even though its forces remain more or less intact.

There may be numerous reasons why an undefeated government should surrender to rebel demands, but all involve a change of mind from an initial determination to resist to an eventual willingness to compromise. Since this change is not occurring at the point of a bayonet, it probably flows from a revised perception of values and priorities. It would seem that something which at the outset was regarded as an asset worth fighting for has become a liability to be dropped. The something might be a policy, a territory, or the right to govern, and the "asset-to-liability shift" may be seen as the objective of the revolutionary psychological attack.

Propaganda is important in all revolutions. Without its aid the leader-ship would be powerless to mobilize the masses, inspire confidence and dedication, and focus hatred. Strategy leading toward a military deci-sion can be strengthened by propaganda that lowers enemy morale and makes rebel victory seem inevitable. Mao Tse-tung, whose revolution-ary theory favored a victory in the field, nevertheless wrote of his campaign: "The Red Army does not make war for war's sake: this is a war of propaganda in the midst of the masses."[13] But for all its impor-tance in this style of struggle, propaganda performs only as a supporting arm. It is in the revolution that relies on the asset-to-liability shift to render government forces irrelevant to the outcome that propaganda becomes the decisive factor, with violence as its handmaiden.

Perhaps the richest seam in which to study propaganda-dominated revolutions is the period of colonial decline, when liberal democracies in the West frequently gave way to international or domestic pressures even though, on the ground, their security forces still retained unbroken power. Ireland after World War I was the archetype, imitated by Menachem Begin in Palestine after the subsequent world conflict,[14] and later by numerous nationalist leaders. The colonial powers had regarded overseas territories as an asset, but after years of guerrilla fighting during which the governments paid dearly in lives, treasure, and domestic and international esteem, these possessions were one by one perceived as liabilities. The Dutch and the French in Indonesia and Indochina respectively lost those territories by force of arms: in virtually every other instance, colonial powers withdrew with their military strength intact but their will to continue the fight broken.

In Vietnam, the Americans suffered a far more damaging defeat by the same process. Here it was not an overseas possession that was converted from asset to liability, but an ideal. The U.S. commitment to defend the South rested upon the value attached to the principle that a friendly noncommunist nation should not be allowed to fall prey to an aggressive communist neighbor. When the cost of upholding this principle became too great, idealism had to be written off as a liability, and in America this has inflicted deep psychological wounds.

The theory of the asset-to-liability shift allows us to understand the role of violence in many low-intensity revolutionary situations. To be sure, the murder of selected individuals, such as police informers and intelligence officers, has a direct tactical purpose, as does the destruction of matériel used by security forces. Such events apart, most violence in situations where the rebels cannot hope to win in open battle is, in Brian Jenkins's words, "aimed at the people watching, not at the actual victims. Terrorism is theatre.''[15] The members of the Provisional I.R.A. were never under the illusion that they could drive the British security forces into the sea. They appreciated from the start that theirs would have to be a campaign of leverage, using the economic, international, and domestic side-effects of their violence on the British public and government to cause the necessary asset-to-liability shift. Propaganda and violence were and are two sides of the same coin.

## Provisional Political and Propaganda Organization

The old IRA, which after the split went under the name "Official," had maintained a political apparatus called Sinn Fein. The Provisionals followed suit, and claimed the same title for what they describe as their "political arm"[16]—a subordinate front organization useful in the evasion of criminal liability, and as an overt propaganda outlet.[17] Real control, political and military, has always been exercised by the IRA Army Council, several of whose members double as political front men in Sinn Fein. Both headquarters are in the Republic of Ireland, in or near Dublin, reflecting national aims. "We are a movement," the Provisionals wrote in 1977, "totally committed to revolution right across the board and from top to bottom. . . ."[18] Dublin is also the home of their "Irish Republican Publicity Bureau," which issues formal press releases under the *nom de guerre* "P. Ó'Néill." The main publication is the weekly *An Phoblacht*, and this is supplemented by pamphlets dealing with separate issues and books summarizing the struggle to date. The sophistication and skill of this activity are well illustrated by Sinn Fein's excellent *Manual of Publicity*,[19] which might provide sound advice to any group seeking to influence public opinion without recourse to expensive advertising.

In Northern Ireland, the sinews of Provisional organization have always been essentially military. Until the late 1970s, elaborate forms borrowed from the 1919–21 struggle were the order of the day, including "brigades," "battalions," "companies," "active service units," and so on, suitable for some form of "people's war," but vulnerable to penetration. Today the IRA is organized on the continental cellular model, appropriate for a purely terroristic campaign, all ideas of a national liberation war having evaporated. Propaganda is dealt with by Sinn Fein and its local publicity offices, and by a network of front spokesmen and apologists: there is political activity at community level, but very little overall policy formulation. Publications such as *Republican News* (now merged with *An Phoblacht)* and *Andersonstown News* give the party line. These formal outlets have been important as the source of inspiration for the committed and to provide points of reference. Each target audience has additionally required its own special treatment, and these are considered now.

## Supporters, Activists, and Volunteers

Both the Catholic and Protestant communities in Northern Ireland have for generations been organized into the types of isolated, self-righteous, and insecure groups that are ideal target audiences for the propagandist.

An organized, closed group can easily strip the individual of his personal identity, replacing his private emotions, beliefs, hopes, and fears
with those approved by the community and articulated by its leaders.
Conformity can be enforced by group dynamics and, if necessary, fear.
We may see, on the one hand, a crack regiment and, on the other, a trade
union as typical examples of such forces at work. In both cases, the rank
and file are usually staunchly loyal to their organization and its mores,
unconscious of the conditioning that has brought them to this state of
mind. Northern Catholics, brought up as the resentful and under-
privileged minority in Protestant Ulster, educated in their own Catholic
schools, joining only Republican sporting and social clubs, attending
only opposition political rallies, and influenced by a Church which
reflected their own fears and aspirations, had from early youth received
what Professor Ellul calls "pre-propaganda," the myths of ancient
battles, of 1916, and the efficacy of violence.[20] Pre-propaganda stan-
dardizes perceptions and reactions, and ensures that, if and when a
certain stimulus is applied, all will respond unhesitatingly along predetermined lines.

It was toward this target audience that the Provisionals applied the
stimulation of their mobilization propaganda. This aimed to turn the
entire Catholic population into close supporters, into Mao's hackneyed
sea fit for rebels to swim in. The same operation would inspire some to
become political activists and act as front spokesmen on behalf of the
movement, and others to enlist as "volunteers" in the IRA proper. As
the activists joined in with words, and the volunteers with bombs and
bullets, the whole creation might take on a life of its own, self-sustaining
and irresistible. By a series of particularly vile murders of off-duty,
unarmed soldiers,[21] the Provisionals began the process of alienating the
Army from Catholics. When in due course it became necessary for the
security forces to conduct house searches for arms, ammunition, and
explosives, a wonderfully effective propaganda campaign convinced
Catholics and a number of journalists that the British were behaving in a
one-sided, anti-Catholic manner, and that they were ham-fisted and
uncaring to boot. This propaganda line was extended to exonerate the
Provisionals, and to blame instead the Protestant establishment, for
"turning the Army around," so that it began to regard the IRA as its
principal enemy.[22]

The campaign was remarkably effective, and it worked, like all strong propaganda, through the interpretation of verifiable *facts*. The righteousness of the cause rested on history, but was sharpened by the recent civil rights activities and their "oppression" by authority. Victory was said to be inevitable, because of the certain triumph of justice. Hatred, that burning essential for revolutionary success, was also conjured out of the past, but as the security forces were drawn into conflict with riotous mobs, organized by the Provisionals, every raised baton, each bruised shoulder, and every arrested man was afterward held up as a victim of gratuitous, partial British brutality.[23] When in August 1971 the British and Northern Ireland governments jointly decided to introduce internment of known and suspected terrorists rather than risk allowing the situation to deteriorate to the point where the Protestants might take the law into their own hands, the first stage of the operation, that took 342 Catholics into arrest, and its propaganda exploitation completed the mobilization of the Catholic masses. "Interrogation in depth," by which the British obtained valuable intelligence from a small number of suspects, but in the process offended their own laws and liberal opinion worldwide, provided ample facts that a novice could have turned to good use, and which the Provisionals and their apologists in the Irish Republic made into a cruelly effective propaganda and political weapon.[24]

While the Catholic masses were made into close supporters, providing safe houses, sealed lips, alert eyes, and instant propaganda in the wake of every incident, the political activists were set in motion. The loose connection between the Provisionals and the SDLP was the most valuable component, but at every level of society fronts played their parts. NICRA was further infiltrated, while other groups, many free of any intended connection with the IRA were manipulated and compromised as opportunity allowed. They included tenants' associations, the Belfast Central Citizens' Defence Committee, the Committee for Truth, the Minority Rights Association, the Association for Legal Justice, the Northern Resistance Movement, and the Anti-Internment League. Certain priests, notably Father Denis Faul of Dungannon, used their pulpits to attack security forces, becoming by this process highly valued and much quoted champions of militant republicanism.

The recruiting of volunteers occurred simultaneously, and these individuals entered a kind of group within a group wherein their indoctrination could be completed by an intensified form of psychological manipulation. This included moral conditioning, necessary to enable young men and women brought up in the Christian faith to perform acts of murder and other crimes. The just war theme, contained in the quotation at the head of this article, was combined with the pretence of formal enlistment into an ''army'' so that recruits were relieved of personal responsibility for their actions. The fact that teen-age boys and girls would hold pistols to their victims' heads, and blow out the brains of people they had never seen before in their lives, or plant bombs in crowded restaurants and bars, knowing the inevitable consequences, testifies to the power of such propaganda, which could only have been effective in so short a time through the conditioning of pre-propaganda. The act of murder, or a lesser crime, consolidated the indoctrination. Compromised beyond withdrawal, having to live with memories that in his or her former life would have been intolerable, the volunteer needed more propaganda to explain and justify the act, and this in turn motivated the next.

## Friends

The next group of audiences was composed of friends throughout the world, who could bring pressure to bear on Britain, directly or indirectly, or raise funds, supply weapons, confuse or misinform public opinion, or otherwise help the cause. This was a mixed bag, and considerable dexterity was needed to supply the appropriate messages to each target, since, as Miss McGuire pointed out, confusion could be dangerous. Of the American audience she wrote:

> . . . visiting speakers . . . were carefully briefed as to how the audience should be played. There should be copious reference to the martyrs of 1916 and 1920–22—the period most of the audience would be living in. Anti-British sentiment, recalling Cromwell, the potato famine, and the Black and Tans, could be profitably exploited. By no means should anything be said against the Catholic Church. And all reference to Socialism should be strictly avoided.[25]

Catholic Irish groups throughout the world were receptive to such messages, and wherever their group cohesion was strong, the propaganda was liable to be effective, moving its audience to *act* rather than merely observe. Outside Ireland, America was the most important target. Senior Provisionals were sent on fund-raising visits to the States very soon after the movement came into being.[26] This activity had two useful purposes: it raised money, and it organized and committed people who were thereafter receptive to propaganda. Irish-Americans so conditioned set up the Irish Northern Aid Committee, generally known as NORAID, which collected funds ostensibly to relieve hardship among Northern Catholics, although in reality most of the money was diverted to buy arms.[27]

In the Irish Republic friends were to be found at all levels of society, wherever the myths and the urge to merge them into present reality overcame pragmatic and moral restraints. The Sinn Fein organization rallied the faithful, and drew in many in support of "our people" in the North who might not have been attracted to the Party in more peaceful times. Newspapers and journals that were editorially opposed to violence nevertheless allowed young militant journalists to cover events in the North and to promote the Provisional cause in their columns. Often, these journalists had one foot in the nationalist camp and another in the next important group of Provisional friends—the radical left.

As a socialist-oriented movement, the Provisionals could count on support from such as the Movement for a Socialist (Irish) Republic, the London-based International Socialists (later to become the Socialist Workers' Party), and the International Marxist Group. These audiences saw the Ulster situation in old-fashioned Marxist terms, of British imperialism and the oppression of the Irish working class. There was the added attraction that a successful revolution in part of the United Kingdom might set a useful precedent for the future. The radical London weekly *Time Out* has published frequent articles helpful to the Provisionals, employing propaganda techniques at once subtle and effective. Elsewhere in Europe the Provisionals have forged links with the revolutionary left in France, West Germany, Italy, Holland, Spain, Austria, and Belgium, benefiting from the work of solidarity committees and laying the groundwork for informal links with terrorist groups in those countries. Libya has welcomed IRA delegates and provided arms, while close links have been formed with the Popular Front for the Liberation of Palestine. While some of this liaison has been for such practical ends as arms procurement, training, and interchange of intelligence, the main benefit in the early years of the struggle was a network of propaganda outlets. Joint operations have been a relatively recent development. To this audience the full radicalism of Provisional ideology is exposed, including justification for the murder of businessmen and plans for the overthrow of the Irish government.

All these leftist sympathizers have tended to belong to the far-out, revolutionary fringe, rather than to the orthodox communist parties, with whom the official IRA has fraternal links. Since, however, it was the Provisionals who led the violence and showed the most capacity to damage British and NATO interests, these parties have been careful not to embarrass or hinder the goose that was laying so golden an egg. In 1972 the Soviet Union sent a *Pravda* correspondent into the Long Kesh internment camp to contact Sean Keenan, a leading Londonderry Provisional, and afterward *Pravda* published a statement calling for worker solidarity with the oppressed Irish people.[28] It is beyond question that the correspondent was an officer in the KGB, and it may have been more than coincidental that the visit was followed within the month by the event in Londonderry that has been called "Bloody Sunday." Aware no doubt of the dangers of openly fermenting revolution within the United Kingdom, the USSR has concentrated its propaganda less in support of Provisional violence than in condemnation of British policy and troops, who, according to one broadcast, "instead of fighting terrorism break up peaceful demonstrations, arrest fighters for civil rights and put them behind bars."[29]

## The Uncommitted

The next audience we need to consider was made up of many diverse groups, consisting, in toto, of all who could possibly influence the outcome of the struggle, but who belonged to neither of the audiences already described, nor to the "enemy." Before mobilization, most Ulster Catholics were in this category, but were gradually won over as supporters and, in the South, there was initially some movement in the same direction. In Britain, the majority were offended by Provisional violence while remaining uncommitted on such questions as Ulster's political future and the role of British troops. Outside the British Isles, Western Europe and North America contained important uncommitted audiences, and the rest of the British Commonwealth and the third world received some attention. Just as supporters, activists, and volunteers sought new recruits from among friends, so friends tried to enlarge their number at the expense of the uncommitted. This, of course, is the pattern of all revolutionary activity, which is distinguished from war between states by the constantly shifting boundaries between all categories. Even the enemy is seen by the true revolutionary as a potential recruit to his own standard.

## The Enemy

Enemies were British troops, and also agents of the Stormont government—whether these were police, prison officers, administrators, or the judiciary—and people responsible for keeping Northern Ireland's economy alive, which could and did include any Protestant who worked in a power station, a public house, a garage, or a shop, in practice the entire one million Protestant majority population. As already observed, Provisional politics ignored this important group, and their propaganda never attempted persuasion. Violent coercion was instead employed, which had the effect of polarizing opinion and making the task of winning Protestant support for some kind of All-Ireland solution more than ever difficult. As for the British troops, the group cohesion of the regimental system effectively insulated them from the few appeals that were directed their way, mainly through indirect channels such as the Marxist "Troops Out" movement and Pat Arrowsmith's "British Withdrawal from Northern Ireland" campaign.

## The Fall of Stormont

Once the internment operation had completed Catholic mobilization, the Provisionals shifted their bombing and sniping campaign into high gear. They were hoping to make Northern Ireland "ungovernable" both in appearance and fact, and thus convert first the Stormont government and ultimately the Province itself from an asset to a liability in the minds of British citizens and their government. Their considerable success in creating mayhem depended for its propaganda payoff upon the support they received from the political and social alliance built around the tactical objective of ending rule from Stormont. This produced an exceptionally effective propaganda barrage, which hit every one of its targets.

In this, the theme of hatred was predominant. It spread its condemnation across the apparatus of "Protestant domination," sparing no one. Northern Ireland politicians were portrayed as racist fascists, the RUC was composed of sadistic bullies, Protestants were, to a man or woman, bigots, and British troops, who so recently had been welcomed as fair-minded saviors, were now blackened as oppressors, torturers, and murderers. Since it was the latter who posed the principal obstacle to IRA attacks, they took the brunt of hatred. Brutality allegations formed the main component of the attack, and front spokesmen of impeccable moral credentials carried allegations to audiences who would never have read *An Phoblacht* or believed the word of an identified IRA spokesman.

The Provisionals drilled their supporters in Catholic areas on their role whenever a shooting incident ended in the death of an IRA volunteer. The man's weapon was to be spirited away and the victim was to be cleaned of forensic evidence indicating that he had handled a gun. "Eye witnesses" would be briefed and presented to journalists. Evidence was never to vary: the dead man would be described as unarmed and innocent of any offense. The soldier's action would be condemned as murder. One journalist who experienced this procedure said:

> I speak as someone of Irish extraction on both sides, yet even I am surprised on occasions at the instant and expert mendacity to which journalists and, no doubt, other interested parties, such as the police and security forces, are treated in episodes of this sort.[30]

Internment of suspects provided fuel for hatred propaganda, since Britain could be shown to be acting "unlawfully" or at least immorally in her "oppression" of Catholic civil rights. The fact that this was a distasteful measure, imposed reluctantly and to be abolished as soon as the security situation allowed, made it difficult to defend, and the theme was ideal for transferring guilt from the perpetrators of violence to those who were trying to oppose it. This was important in the undermining of British public opinion, which had anyway inherited a guilt complex over Ireland, and which was always happier when acting the part of David (the Spanish Armada, Napoleon, Mons, the Battle of Britain) than of Goliath. The purpose of Provisional propaganda directed at Britain, and at most uncommitted audiences, was less to convert than to confuse and embarrass. By creating doubts, minds that were determined might be changed. If the man on the Clapham omnibus began to wonder whether his troops were indeed misbehaving, and whether the law was being abused, and whether government policy was sectarian and unjust, then he would worry. If, on top of these fears, he could be made to doubt whether security measures were achieving any useful results, whether in fact the campaign that was costing so many lives could ever be brought to a successful conclusion, then he might easily revise his earlier support for a policy of resistance.

Propaganda therefore sought to prove the hopelessness as well as the brutality of security measures, using such themes as the "long war," which argues that time is on the side of the rebels because as long as there is one insurgent left the revolution will continue, and since the government obviously cannot eliminate every volunteer and activist, they cannot ever hope to win; "justified reaction," which insists that the revolutionary violence is merely an unavoidable reaction to in-stitutionalized violence by the state; "security force incompetence," which shows troops and police to be blundering about in the dark, arresting the innocent and shooting the blameless, while the rebels are too clever to be caught; and, carried over from mobilization propaganda and reinforced by these themes of doubt, the "inevitable triumph" of the revolution.

None of these themes could be convincing without *facts* to back them up, and this is where propaganda depended upon violent action, upon "propaganda by the deed." The murder of a soldier or the blowing up of a hotel provided evidence of the movement's capability, unimpaired by anything that authority could do, and the sufferings of Catholics in areas where street fighting occurred, searches were carried out, and arrests made, were displayed without reference to the terrorist acts which had preceded them. Facts, in most cases created by violence, had another vital purpose: they made news.

Within the organized groups of friends and supporters, propaganda media such as face-to-face persuasion, handbills, leaflets, the move-ment's publications, meetings, loudspeakers, and of course *terror* were effective. Beyond these boundaries, these homespun methods had almost no effect. There was one means and one means only to reach out to the uncommitted—the news media. Since Provisional strategy de-pended for its hope of success on reaching these distant audiences, the media became, whether they liked it or not, the vital ground over which the key component of the struggle was fought. The Provisionals appreciated this fact better than their opponents. Moreover the civil rights campaign of the late 1960s had attracted media sympathy for Catholic causes and almost completely destroyed the reputation and credibility of Stormont and the RUC. Even journalists who were totally opposed to Provisional violence tended to support the "smash Stormont" objective. This ambivalence, reinforced by liberal trends and the Vietnam syndrome, placed many influential reporters in a nonaligned or neutralist position from which they judged the actions of terrorists and security forces in a moral vacuum.[31]

News is built upon events, and spectacular events make headlines. Murders and explosions tended therefore to catch the readers' eyes, while reports of security force successes were more often than not limited to dry announcements, circumscribed by legal and other constraints, that certain individuals had been arrested in connection with some offence. The electronic media, particularly television, magnified this tendency. Thus the casual observer's perception of the conflict was molded by images and messages which tended to reinforce the themes of doubt discussed earlier. The Provisionals certainly understood this process. When in November 1971 the Army stole the headlines by arresting two much-wanted Provisionals, Martin Meehan and Dutch Docherty, the IRA in Londonderry called the London Press Association with a plausible but false story designed to overshadow the arrests. McGuire tells us how the Provisionals set off bombs in Belfast to coincide with a press conference called by the general commanding the British troops, both to upstage his remarks and to capture headlines.[32]

A continued high level of violence strengthened Provisional credibility, which is a measure of apparent military prowess, while mass Catholic support for the struggle and international concern over alleged British wrongs of policy and implementation raised Provisional legitimacy, which is the revolutionary's claim to loyalty and obedience. When a movement can assemble massive stocks of credibility and legitimacy, it may be close to achieving its political goals. By early 1972 the Provisional IRA had in fact been severely weakened by security force action and was beginning to lose the confidence of its supporters, so much so that it found it necessary to retreat from full-scale terrorist attacks and return to the earlier tactic of galvanizing the Catholic population into taking to the streets in riotous assemblies that the police and military would be forced to confront. IRA propaganda hid the movement's weakness from uncommitted audiences,[33] while agents of influence in Britain persuaded some members of the Labor Party opposition, and a number of trade union officials, that, as the "military solution" had clearly failed to end the violence, the time had come for military action to be replaced by a "political initiative." No one doubted that, if such an initiative were deemed necessary, it would have to be launched by the Westminster government, and would therefore mark the end of the Stormont regime. While these possibilities were being discussed, an IRA-inspired civil rights march in Londonderry ended in a shootout between British troops and gunmen hidden in an apartment block, and 13 Catholics, mostly free of guilt, were killed in the mêlée.[34] Not surprisingly, the event sent shock waves through Ireland and Britain, and they hit Europe and America with undiminished force. This was precisely the sort of tragedy the Provisionals needed, and had possibly planned, and in one day they recovered with compound interest all the grass-roots support they had lost, and their legitimacy soared. In Britain, doubts became certainties. The value that had been attached to continued government of the Province by Stormont shrank below zero and that institution was seen as a liability. Two months after Bloody Sunday the British government prorogued Stormont and assumed "direct rule" over Northern Ireland. The Catholic social and political alliance had achieved its major objective, and the Provisionals had reached their first tactical goal.

With hindsight it is easy to see that the British government had chosen to fight its initial encounter with the Provisionals on the wrong ground. By defending a Stormont regime that it neither trusted nor wholeheartedly supported, it exposed British policy to criticism of partial support for the Protestant majority, and of assisting the "oppression" of minority Catholics, without gaining the benefit of a fully mobilized majority population behind the counterinsurgency effort. Of course, it is understandable that no Westminster government wished to embark on a so drastic and in its way antidemocratic course as the ending of provincial government, but it would obviously have been far less damaging to do this early, as a chosen act of policy, rather than later, in reluctant response to violence. The social, political, and military alliance might never have come into being, the Catholic masses might not have been mobilized in support of violence, and Britain's reputation for giving in to terrorism might not have been further embellished, if the Provisionals had been denied so popular a cause to champion.

April 1972 was a month of hope and opportunity in Catholic Ireland, and for Protestants, in spite of the resentment and fears aroused by direct rule, there was at least the prospect of peace. The Provisionals were presented with that "hole in the sky"—a rare and fleeting opportunity that rational revolutionaries are ready to respond to—through which they can move from violence into politics. Here was a British Minister in Ulster ready and willing to negotiate, a Royal Air Force VIP plane put at the Army Council's disposal, partnership in the Province's political future for the asking. To be sure, the British were not offering a united Ireland: this did not lie within their power to give. They offered a return to the peaceful process of reconciliation between North and South, between Protestant and Catholic, that had prospered in the 1960s until shattered by the impatience of radical students and civil rights activists, and they made clear their willing acceptance of a united Ireland should a majority in the Province prefer this solution. It is difficult to imagine how respect for democracy and the rights of Protestants could be reconciled with any more dynamic proposals.

## Campaign for a United Ireland

The Provisional leadership may have misread Westminster's willingness to yield over Stormont and readiness to negotiate over the future as signs of a general collapse of will, or they may have been psychologically unable to make the transition from violence to politics.

We live, as Ellul points out,[35] in an age when means far outstrip ends and aims. It is easier to do things than explain motives, and by moving quickly from one action to the next, explanations can be deferred indefinitely. People and groups that fall into this habit, as Hitler and his Nazi party did throughout their terrible era, are apt to become addicted, so that in the end actions—violent actions—become their sole motive and justification. Whatever the cause, the Provisionals ran scared from the prospect of peace, and threw themselves into the tasks of destroying the peace movement that had sprung up among Catholic women,[36] persuading their erstwhile supporters and activists to transfer their energies to the strategic goal of a united Ireland, and intensifying the violence against Protestants and troops. Their propaganda warned of the dangers of giving up when victory was in sight, after so many had died in the struggle, and it sought to reassure Northern Catholics that the Protestant paramilitary forces that had begun to form in the wake of Stormont's demise were "paper tigers." As these themes failed, they were increasingly replaced by the simple coercion of terror. SDLP leaders denounced the senseless slayings with the same courage that had distinguished their campaign against Stormont, and came under verbal and physical attack from the Provisionals. Catholics, afraid that British protection might soon be withdrawn, dreaded both the terrorists in their midst and the Protestant revenge that might be just around the corner. They continued to accept the devil they knew, but their vocal and material support faded. The social, political, and military alliance was ended: henceforth the Provisionals were on their own.

In their frustrated fury, the Provisionals struck out wildly, killing Protestants in an apparent effort to intimidate that community into surrender. On July 21, 1972 their volunteers mounted a massive bomb attack in Belfast. Within 70 minutes 22 explosions killed eleven people. TV crews were soon at the scenes of these crimes and the reports that sped down the wires to the news capitals of the world seemed to convince many TV editors, and certainly those in Britain, that they could no longer remain neutral toward such events. They therefore decided to show the horrific consequences to a public halfway persuaded to think of bomb attacks as romantic, Robin Hood-style adventures. What they witnessed on their color screens inspired a remarkably frank editorial in the Dublin *Sunday Independent:*

> We fostered the men who planned the murders of innocent men, women, boys and girls in Belfast on Friday. We fed these people with propaganda. We took advantage, when we could, of their exploits . . . Now all of us must pay the price for this neglect.[37]

After "Bloody Friday," Provisional propaganda leaned heavily on themes of justification and of survival. Instead of stressing the righteousness of their cause—which was impossible in the circumstances— the evil of the enemy became the main sustaining theme. Hatred was focused on any part of the security apparatus that posed a severe threat to their freedom of action, so that murders would be justified in advance of the act. As the overall security situation in Northern Ireland improved, and the Royal Ulster Constabulary began to resume its proper function, this force became the prime target in place of the Army. The campaign alleged that police officers systematically brutalized IRA suspects, particularly during interrogation. Carefully staged interviews between alleged victims and ideologically-motivated journalists produced the "case histories" necessary to bring the allegations to life. Once published, such material would attract interest from the rest of the media and the theme would become a "story" or "issue." Television and radio personalities would pick it up, and the hasty and shallow style of their research made them easy for the Provisonals to influence. The media not only provided false justification for the murders of policemen; the leader of the Police Federation of Northern Ireland has claimed that on one occasion a television program actually led directly to such a murder.[38] Independent inquiries subsequently exposed the falsity of the brutality campaign[39] but, by the nature of propaganda, it is the first story that is believed, and truth is anyway a poor substitute for sensation.

For all that, it made a wonderful propaganda target; internment was in one respect an arrangement welcomed by Provisionals and Protestant extremists alike. By excluding the courts and sentencing procedure, it resembled capture in battle. Internees were, in a sense, prisoners of war, who could confidently expect their freedom in exchange for some truce, amnesty, or settlement. Such a hope is vital for the morale of volunteers and their families, and for the recruiting of replacements. After internment was ended, more and more Provisionals went before courts and received long sentences for their crimes—a trend intensified after various bombing attacks in Britain ended in arrests. The risk of death in the course of an operation has never been too severe a deterrent among people educated to admire martyrdom, but thirty years in prison make for an altogether different prospect. To overcome this psychological barrier, the Provisionals launched campaigns demanding "special status" for convicted prisoners. Because the true purpose of this theme was scarcely likely to appeal outside the ranks of committed supporters, it had to be dressed up for wider audiences, particularly in the United States. Hence the "H Block" operation.

# Propaganda in the United States

The campaign was mounted by a special "H-Block Appeal Fund" set up at Provisional Sinn Fein headquarters in Dublin and supported by an "H-Block Information Center" in the Falls Road, Belfast. Their U.S. office was NORAID, New York. Themes originated in *An Phoblacht/ Republican News* and were picked by such dedicated outlets in the United States as *Irish People,* which on December 9, 1978 alleged that, "Long Kesh [the Maze prison in Northern Ireland] presages a holocaust that would lead to further strife and bloodshed" and insisted that prisoners convicted of murder and attempted murder, firearms and explosives offenses should be treated as "political prisoners."[40] To strengthen this theme with "human interest," IRA prisoners refused to wear clothes, covering themselves instead with blankets, destroyed furniture, smeared their cell walls with excreta, and refused to wash. As intended, their conditions worsened, and, when prison staff attempted to intervene, their actions were portrayed as brutality. Provisional terrorists meanwhile murdered as many off-duty prison staff as they were able, so as to bring a two-edged psychological weapon to bear. The theme, now dressed as a "news story" was picked up by sympathetic or misinformed journalists such as Ed Blanche, Associated Press's Belfast correspondent,[41] and then by such respected newsmen as Jack Anderson.[42] When the story began to fade, support groups brought Father Raymond Murray from Armagh to New York, and his contribution led to some colorful coverage.[43] Next to arrive was Ciaran Nugent, a Provisional recently released from Maze prison, who performed before news cameras and spoke the appropriate words. The *Irish Echo* saw Nugent as a latter-day Tom Paine or Nathan Hale,[44] and his allegations received coverage in *The Advocate,*[45] the *Philadelphia Inquirer,*[46] the *Philadelphia Daily News,*[47] and many other papers including, of course, Pete Hamill's column in the *New York Daily News.*[48] The importation of these Provisional spokesmen involved money and that indispensable element in propaganda—organization.

By the mid-1970s NORAID's arms-purchasing activities had been so well documented[49] that the organization could no longer posture as a charitable group. It continued its work, but other fronts were created or infiltrated to lead in the propaganda field. Prime among the new creations was the Washington-based Irish National Caucus (INC). Although unashamedly devoted to IRA terrorism,[50] its sponsors appreciated the impossibility of gaining widespread American support for murder and other atrocities committed by a movement that represented only some two percent of Irishmen.[51] Therefore, it sought to help the Provisionals by attacking their enemies—the British government, the RUC, and any counterinsurgency technique (such as imprisonment of convicts) that lowered terrorists' morale. Their theme was cunningly selected, since as a "motherhood" buzzword it was above criticism—"Human Rights." These rights did not include the right to life itself for any who opposed the Provisionals, or who were selected as "symbolic targets," or indeed for any who happened to be in the vicinity of some IRA attack, such as the twelve civilians incinerated in a restaurant on February 17, 1978, the 69-year-old woman shot dead in a soccer crowd, or the 10-year-old girl blown to pieces in a booby-trapped car. Stripped of its fantasy, the INC's propaganda sponsored one right only—the right of the Provisionals to murder at will, without fear of retribution or condemnation.

The INC's original director was Sean Walsh, a one-time Green Beret who was registered under the Foreign Agents' Registration Act as the U.S. representative of Provisional Sinn Fein.[52] However, in 1978 the Bishop of Corpus Christi, Texas, the Most Reverend Dr. Thomas Drury, set up a special "Ministry of Peace and Justice for Ireland" consisting of Father Sean McManus, who was to work as the INC's chief activist in Washington.[53] Asked in 1975 by a British television reporter if he supported the Provisional IRA, McManus had said: "I do, yes. I'm on record for quite a long time now for supporting the Provisional IRA."[54]

McManus proved a tireless and effective activist, providing by his cloth the saintly glow of righteousness and by his rhetoric the smoke screen of misinformation, doubt, and ambiguity behind which the Provisionals could operate. The INC drew support from the long-established Ancient Order of Hibernians in America, and that organization set up a "Political Education Committee" to carry INC messages to widespread audiences.[55] McManus also worked with Bill Bartnett's American Irish Congress, a lobbying vehicle to "apply pressure on candidates"[56] and other groups such as the Catholic Lawyers for Human Rights, the AFL-CIO Labor Council for Human Rights in Northern

Ireland, the American Irish Institute, and Tom Duffy's Irish News Service.

His strongest ally, however, was Congressman Mario Biaggi. Biaggi created the Ad-Hoc Congressional Committee for Irish Affairs in 1977, by the imaginative trick of inviting all Congressmen with Irish-American electors to join and thus demonstrate their concern over Irish affairs (and Irish votes). Scarcely any dared to refuse and, although few of these individuals had any sympathy for Provisional terrorism, by their act of membership they were mobilized into a powerful political pressure group, easily manipulated by Biaggi.[57] In his end-of-the-year statement for 1979,[58] which the Congressman described as a "productive year," Biaggi measured the Ad Hoc Committee's success by efforts which had led in early August to a suspension of U.S. small-arms sales to the RUC. He also spoke of having raised the Irish issue from a position of relative obscurity to one which now enjoys national and international visibility. The means employed by the Provisionals to "raise their visibility" was murder, most notably the late August killing of Lord Mountbatten, his 14-year old grandson, and another boy, and the 82-year old Dowager Lady Brabourne, but also of many soldiers, policemen, and casual victims. Of these two events, the arms embargo and the killings, the London *Economist* wrote:

The killers were partly financed by citizens of the United States, and most informed Britons thought that the Carter administration's decision four weeks ago to delay arms sales to Ulster's police (so as to please some Irish American voters) would encourage the IRA into another murderous heave. This last effort was not merely forecastable, it was forecast.[59]

The Mountbatten family carnage rebounded on the Provisionals and opened many uncommitted eyes to the true nature of Irish terrorism. Sean Patrick Walsh attempted to excuse the murders, applying the theme of "justified reaction," and sought to reassure Americans that the Provisionals represented the great mass of Irish people,[60] a proposition which most Irish would find disgusting.

Thomas McMahon, the man who made and planted the sophisticated remote-controlled bomb that killed Mountbatten, had reportedly been trained by the KGB in Libya.[61] If this was indeed the case, we have

witnessed an extraordinary alliance of orthodox communism, the Islamic revolutionary left, and militant Irish America. Within its narrow,
tactical limits, this must be acknowledged as a triumph of Provisional
propaganda.


## Strategic Prospects

Between the Soviet Union, which knows what it is doing, and Irish
America, which does not, the Provisionals are supplied with arms,
skills, money, and political support. The Soviets doubtless relish an
unstable Ireland and a weakened NATO: they may also value further
opportunities to experiment in what Gerald Holton calls Type III terrorism, or terrorism "which disrupts personal and historic memory
through large-scale catastrophe organized for that purpose" by states in
collusion with groups.[62] Irish-Americans, militant and level-headed
alike, generally favor a united Ireland, and this aspiration enjoys qual-
ified a support in the Irish Republic. Present political patterns, however,
seem far more likely to favor Soviet ambitions than those involving
unity. Provisional hopes of achieving their strategic goal appear still to
rest on coercing Britain into delivering this prize. This writer takes the
view that had it been within Britain's ability during the past eleven years
to find some formula for escaping further involvement in Northern
Ireland, she would in all probability have cut her losses and quit. It is
extremely unlikely that many in government, even in 1969, saw Northern Ireland as a political, economic, or strategic asset, and it is more
unlikely still that anyone sees the Province in that light now. Consequently, the theory of the asset-to-liability shift has no application in its
ordinary form. War weariness, and the fear that an existing liability may
become intolerable to bear, could create leverage on government to pull
out, but in the decision-making process the probable conclusion would
be that, bad though continued resistance might be (and right now it is
not particularly onerous), the likely consequences of a precipitous
withdrawal would be far worse *for Britain,* never mind Ireland. Our
memories are short when we wish to forget, but Beirut's 40,000 dead
should give us pause for thought. America's refusal to consider the
Palestinians in 1947 has left a painful heritage, and any reluctance to

acknowledge Protestant civil rights in Ireland today could lead to some similar legacy. Already one leftist state, Libya, has foreseen the disruptive potential of a bitter, betrayed, and besieged minority in an Ireland where political patterns had been overturned by violence.[63] As for the Republic, the prospect of governing one million Northern rebels might provide a new twist to Wolf Tone's dictum that Ireland unfree will never be at peace.

It may be sensible to concede that Ireland can be united in any constructive and lasting sense only by the will of the majority of Northern Protestants, and to conclude that the restoration of peace must therefore be the first priority. Terrorism and the themes of hatred hamper progress: indeed every year of violence makes the task of persuading the North to join a united Ireland more difficult. The myths of Catholic Ireland and the pretence that one million Protestants are not an important factor, both of which are being eroded in the Irish Republic[64] but remain strong in Irish America, act as psychological barriers to the imaginative initiative which may be needed. Provisional propaganda and the politics of violence between them compose the greatest obstacle to unity, and as such testify to the bankruptcy of that movement's philosophy.

## Notes

1. Peter J. Villiers, "Where Angels Fear to Tread: An Excursion into Irish Politics," in *Journal of the Royal United Services Institute for Defence Studies,* Vol. 124, No. 3 (London, 1979).

2. P. Ó'Néill (nom de plume), Foreword to *Freedom Struggle,* Irish Republican Publicity Bureau (Provisional IRA) (Dublin, 1973).

3. See, for instance, Constantine Fitzgibbon, *Out of the Lion's Paw: Ireland Wins her Freedom* (London, 1969).

4. *Constitution of Ireland,* (July 1, 1937, as amended September, 1939, May 30, 1941), Art 2. "The national territory consists of the whole island of Ireland, its islands and the territorial seas."

5. P. Ó'Néill op. cit., pp. 94–96, and Ruairi O. Bradaigh, "Restore Power to the People," in *The Guardian Weekly,* February 24, 1980, p. 5.

6. See Julian Paget, *Last Post: Aden 1963–67* (London, 1969).

7. See Peter Braestrup, *Big Story: How the American Press and Television*

*Reported and Interpreted the Crisis of Tet 1968 in Vietnam and Washington* (2 vols.) (Boulder, U.S.A., 1977).

8. Maria McGuire, *To Take Arms* (London, 1973), pp. 69–70.

9. See, for instance, Warren B. Wells and N. Marlowe, *A History of the Irish Rebellion of 1916* (Dublin and London, 1916), and Conor Cruise O'Brien, *States of Ireland* (London, 1972).

10. See Charles Townshend, *The British Campaign in Ireland 1919–1921* (Oxford, 1975).

11. McGuire, op. cit., pp. 103–104.

12. See Insight Team, *Ulster* (London, 1972), Chapter 9.

13. Quoted in Jacques Ellul, *Propaganda: The Formation of Men's Attitudes* (New York, 1965), p. 306.

14. See Menachem Begin, *The Revolt* (Los Angeles, 1948).

15. Brian M. Jenkins, "International Terrorism: A New Mode of Conflict," in *International Terrorism and World Security* (London, 1975), p. 16.

16. P. Ó'Néill, op. cit., p. v.

17. For an explanation of the relationship between overt and covert wings of revolutionary organization, see Frank Kitson, *Low Intensity Operations* (London, 1971), Chapter 6.

18. Quoted in *An Phoblacht* (Dublin, October 26, 1977).

19. Provisional Sinn Fein, *Manual of Publicity* (not for public sale or distribution) (Meitheamh, 1974).

20. See Ellul, op. cit., p. 62–79.

21. Insight, op. cit., p. 249.

22. The Insight Team evidently swallowed this theme. See op. cit., Chapter 12. A more balanced account appears in Conor Cruise O'Brien, op. cit., pp. 244–45.

23. In a letter to the *Sunday Telegraph* (London, November 28, 1971) Miss Honor Tracy wrote: "The charitable might say that the Irish tend not to minimize their sufferings; the candid that they are shocking old cry babies . . . nothing that happens, no action of troops or police, relates in any way to anything done by themselves. . . ."

24. On January 18, 1978, the European Court of Human Rights ruled by 13 votes to 4 that "the five techniques did *not* constitute a practice of torture." *Times* (London, January 19, 1978). But that time, however, the damage to Britain's reputation had been done.

25. McGuire, op. cit., pp. 103–104.

26. Ibid., pp. 31–32.

27. See Patrick Cooney, quoted in *Irish Press* (Dublin, February 23, 1974).

28. Reported in *Irish Times* (Dublin, January 21, 1972). The Soviets had

earlier attempted to supply arms to the Provisionals, but the consignment was seized by Dutch police.

29. *Moscow Radio* (January 10, 1976).

30. Tony Geraghty, quoted in RUSI, *Ten Years of Terrorism* (London, 1979), p. 108.

31. See Institute for Conflict Studies, *Television and Conflict* (London, 1978); John Terraine, Martin Bell and Robin Walsh, "Terrorism and the Media," in RUSI, op. cit.; and Yonah Alexander (ed.), "Terrorism and the Media," *Terrorism: An International Journal,* Vol. 2, Nos. 1, 2 (New York, 1979).

32. McGuire, op. cit., p. 75.

33. See, for instance, report by Simon Winchester, "Provisional IRA in Confident Mood," *Guardian* (Manchester, December 20, 1971) as an example of how wool was pulled over journalists' eyes.

34. See Parliament, *Report of the Tribunal appointed to inquire into the events 30 January 1972, which led to loss of life in connection with the Procession in Londonderry that Day* (The Widgery Tribunal) (London, 1972).

35. Ellul, op. cit., p. 195.

36. This was a small, spontaneous movement, which predated the stronger "Peace Movement" of the mid 1970s.

37. *Sunday Independent* (Dublin, July 23, 1972).

38. *Irish Independent* (March 15, 1977). See also, the leader "The BBC's Irish Troubles" *The Times* (March 16, 1977).

39. See the *Bennett Report* and statement by the Chief Constable, Sir Kenneth Newman, in *Constabulary Gazette,* Vol. 44, No. 4 (Belfast, April 1979).

40. John C. McGee, Head of the American Committee for Irish Human Rights, in *Irish People* (New York, December 9, 1978). ·

41. Ed Blanche, "IRA Hygiene Strike in Jail: 3 Years of Locked Wills," in *International Herald Tribune* (January 20/21, 1979).

42. Jack Anderson, "Mystery shrouds Northern Ireland prison," in *Westchester Daily Times* (Westchester, February 11, 1979).

43. See, for instance, George Souza, "Irish Chaplain reveals jail horrors," in *Herald American* (April 29, 1979); Colman McCarthy, "Victims in Northern Ireland," in *Washington Post* (Washington, May 16, 1979); Pete Hamill "Northern Ireland's pain becomes excruciating in jails," in *New York Daily News* (New York, May 14, 1979); "Dialogue," in *National Catholic Register* (Los Angeles, June 3, 1979).

44. *Irish Echo* (New York, August 25, 1979).

45. *The Advocate* (New York, August 25, 1979).

46. *Philadelphia Inquirer* (Philadelphia, August 17, 1979).

47. *Philadelphia Daily News* (Philadelphia, August 13 and 16, 1979).

48. *New York Daily News* (New York, August 13, 1979).

49. See, for instance, Bernard Weintraub, "Bronx IRA Aid Unit Linked to Arms Flow," in *New York Times* (New York, December 16, 1975).

50. See Sean Cronin, "Biaggi stands up for the Provisionals," in *Irish Times* (Dublin, April 28, 1975), and Prime Minister Lynch quoted in *Time* (New York, November 12, 1979), p. 54.

51. Estimate of Provisional Sinn Fein support offered by Keith Kyle, "How Hopeless is the Irish Problem?" in *Encounter* (London, February, 1980).

52. Bernard Weinraub, "Lobby Linked to IRA Asserts It's Gaining Support in Congress," in *New York Times* (New York, September 21, 1979).

52. *Irish News* (Dublin, December 20, 1978).

54. Weinraub (Sept. 21, 1979), op. cit.

55. *The Advocate* (New York, March 1, 1980).

56. See *Irish Echo* (New York, February 9, 1980).

57. *Time,* op. cit.

58. *The Advocate* (New York, December 22, 1979).

59. *Economist* (London, September 1, 1979).

60. Sean Patrick Walsh, "To England: Leave Ireland," in *New York Times* (New York, November 8, 1979).

61. See box in Keith Kyle, op. cit., quoting *Daily Mail*. "The instruction could alternatively have been arranged by the two renegade Americans, previously members of the CIA, who have been indicted by a federal grand jury in Washington for allegedly selling their services to Qaddifi's terror school. [see *MacLean's* (Toronto, June 23, 1980)]. Nevertheless, KGB assistance to the Provisional IRA was exposed as early as 1971 when a four-ton consignment of Czech arms destined for the Provisionals was seized by Dutch authorities at Schipol airport. Moreover, Qaddifi's sponsorship of the Munich massacre and the OPEC ministers' kidnapping by groups trained and otherwise assisted by the KGB (Carlos is a Moscow graduate) reveals an unstructured but effective link between the Islamic fanatic and the Soviet pragmatists."

62. See Gerald Holton, "Reflections on Modern Terrorism," in *Terrorism: An International Journal,* Vol. 1, Nos. 3, 4 (New York, 1978).

63. See *Belfast Telegraph* (Belfast, November 15, and December 4, 1974) and *Times* (London, April 22, 1975).

64. See Kevin Byrne, "Attacking Irish Myths of Violence," in *MacLeans* (Toronto, January 14, 1980).

# The Water and the Fish: Public Opinion and the Provisional IRA in Northern Ireland

E. Moxon-Browne

Department of Political Science
Queen's University of Belfast
Belfast, Northern Ireland

*Abstract*        The methods and goals of the Provisional IRA make it difficult to categorize it simply as a "terrorist" group. Its longevity and its affinity to Irish political culture suggest that it will not be defeated by force but by being rendered irrelevant. This is likely to come about as a result of the state demonstrating its own legitimacy among those sections of the Catholic community which have been understandably reluctant to give the state their full allegiance in the past. Survey evidence supports the contention that the Provisional IRA's goals and grievances are shared by many who would spurn their tactics.

## Introduction

A leading exponent of the concept of "political terrorism" has argued that it is characterized, above all, by "amorality and antinomianism."[1] In other words, the political terrorist regards himself as exempt from existing moral codes because the political goals which he seeks to achieve justify the methods he uses. It follows, therefore, that in many cases an act of political terrorism will be arbitrary, indiscriminate, and unpredictable to those who are its actual or potential victims.

However careful we are in defining terrorism or terrorists we cannot escape making something of a subjective judgment. It is because someone is "terrorized" by an act that the act itself becomes a terrorist act, and its perpetrator a terrorist. Yet an element of randomness or unpredictability is also a vital ingredient in the definition, since the timid driver who is "terrified" when the policeman stops him to give him a ticket, does not automatically regard the policeman as a terrorist! Legitimacy is another ingredient, albeit subjective, in our judgment of whether someone is a terrorist. The familiar argument as to whether members of a certain group are "terrorists" or "liberation fighters" revolves around the perceived legitimacy of the group in question. The distinction between terrorism and guerrilla warfare can become blurred in the public mind when efforts are made by the state to discredit guerrillas by calling them terrorists.

In the light of these preliminary remarks, it is not easy to label the Provisional IRA (PIRA) a terrorist group and leave it at that. The IRA has waged a campaign of intermittent violence in Ireland for about sixty years. Its resilience and longevity, if nothing else, make it exceptional in European terms. But its view of itself as "the legitimate Republic" and its belief that the Dublin government (to say nothing of British rule in Northern Ireland) is a gross usurpation, distinguish it sharply from other subversive groups in Europe like ETA, the Brigate Rosse, the Baader-Meinhof gang, and the South Moluccans, none of whom can lay claim to the sort of ancestry which purports to make them the true repository of the nation's honor. And it is easier to describe these other European groups as terroristic since their campaigns tend to be spasmodic, irrational and, apparently, devoid of widespread support. On the other hand, the IRA displays some of the characteristics of a guerrilla movement, and it is instructive to reflect on Wilkinson's distinction between "guerrillas" and "terrorists":

> Guerrillas may fight in small numbers and with often inadequate weaponry, but they can and often do fight according to conventions of war, taking and exchanging prisoners and respecting the rights of non-combatants. Terrorists place no limits on means employed and frequently resort to widespread assassination, the waging of "general terror" upon the indigenous civilian population. . . .[2]

The present campaign of PIRA does not fall wholly into either of these categories. Certainly, even those most hostile to PIRA find no difficulty in seeing their campaign as essentially a guerrilla campaign;[3] and certainly PIRA sees itself as an "army" fighting a war against an alien power in order to achieve "national liberation."

However, if we return to Wilkinson's conception of "political terrorism," we find that the PIRA campaign falls quite easily into his third category which he calls "revolutionary terrorism" (the other two being "repressive terrorism" and "sub-revolutionary terrorism"),[4] whose main characteristics are:

> Always a group phenomenon, however tiny the group, with a leadership and an ideology or programme, however crude. Develops alternative institutional structures. The organisation of violence and terrorism is typically undertaken by specialist conspiratorial and paramilitary organs within the revolutionary movement.[5]

Even if it is accepted that the PIRA indulges in a form of "revolutionary terrorism" as described here, the tactics are classic guerrilla tactics. PIRA is inusual in engaging in both rural and urban guerrilla warfare with equal success, although in the current campaign the emphasis is on the urban areas and, even outside those areas, there is a tendency to concentrate on the dislocation of inter-urban communications. The theorists of guerrilla warfare argue the merits of rural and urban campaigns[6] but, for the IRA, the memories of the desolate border campaign (1956–62) are probably enough to settle the argument.

In sum, then, although the term "terrorist" is widely used to describe PIRA, especially in Northern Ireland, it is important to keep in mind the differences between PIRA and other groups in Europe which are similarly described. The term "terrorist" has obvious pejorative overtones, and is a natural weapon in the armory of the state as it seeks to discredit its opponents. The "criminalization" of a campaign which is, to some extent, politically inspired is a theme we shall return to later because it is part of the battle for legitimacy between the state and those who wish to overturn the state.

## Development of PIRA

The origins of PIRA lie in the split of the IRA into two wings in 1969–70 over tactics. This split arose from a growing divergence of views over what the appropriate response should be to the civil rights campaign in the North. The Official IRA (OIRA), as it became known, had been strongly influenced by the aims of the civil rights campaign; also by the need to tackle problems like unemployment, bad housing, and so on, in the South. The virtual abandonment of the Catholic ghettoes to face Protestant attackers in 1969–70, and the taunting gable-end slogans "IRA = I Ran Away" that followed, marked the parting of the ways. The OIRA called a cease-fire in 1972, but PIRA went over to the offensive and, except for some short-lived "cease-fires," have held the initiative ever since.

To understand the stance of PIRA since 1972, it is necessary to recapitulate, albeit briefly, the earlier history of the IRA from which PIRA now considers itself to be the true descendant.[7] In general terms, the IRA was born out of the struggle to rid Ireland of British rule. The first attempt to establish a 32-county republic—in 1916—failed, and it was not until January 4, 1922 that the relationship between Britain and Ireland was redefined—an agreement which was accepted by the Dail by 64 votes to 57. Henceforth, Ireland became the Free State but there still remained links with Britain—a Governor-General, an oath to the Crown for TDs, and some concessions over military bases for Britain. The 1921 Government of Ireland Act which gave the six northern counties their own parliament was regarded as a betrayal of the "Republic" by the IRA who responded with a brief, but ultimately futile, campaign.

DeValera's Sinn Fein party contested the 1923 elections and refused to take its seats. Finding abstentionism unproductive, De Valera formed the Fianna Fail Party in 1926, won 44 seats in the 1927 elections, then entered the Dail but refused to take the Oath. In the meantime, the IRA continued to pose a subversive threat and this was reflected in the need to pass special legislation: the Public Safety Act (1923) and the Juries Protection Bill (1929).

Continuing violence from the IRA in the 1930s was a constant reminder that it claimed to represent the "real Republic," a claim which still found some sympathy among the public at large. After 1932, De Valera tried to emasculate the IRA further by a policy of absorption. The Special Branch became staffed by ex-IRA men; and a volunteer militia was set up to give potential IRA members regular pay and a uniform to wear. As Bowyer Bell puts it: "Old grievances were transformed into new loyalties to the government.'[8] On the constitutional side, De Valera endeavored to create something resembling the "real Republic." The Governor-General was replaced by an obscure Fianna Fail politician. Land annuities were no longer paid to the British government, and in 1937 a new Constitution omitted any mention of the Crown and defined the national territory as the 32 counties. This policy of mollifying the IRA could not be carried much further, but it still failed to satisfy hard-core Republicans who sought an end to partition—something which De Valera himself recognized could not be achieved by force.

Thus, by 1939 the IRA had been partly crushed and partly absorbed into Fianna Fail. The Second World War, however, gave the IRA the chance to harass Britain over the question of partition and a campaign was launched in Britain which culminated in an incident in Coventry where five people died and 60 were injured. At the same time, De Valera cracked down harder on the IRA in Ireland. The Offences Against the State Act was passed in 1939; military tribunals tried IRA suspects of whom hundreds were interned in the Curragh. By the end of the war, the IRA was seriously weakened by this constant harassment and its principal raison d'être, the problem of partition, showed no sign of being resolved.

Fianna Fail showed that it sympathized with the aspirations of the IRA, if not with its methods, when it mounted an international publicity campaign on the partition issue in the postwar period. In 1948, The Republic of Ireland Act, passed by a coalition of Fine Gael and Clann na Poblachta, made it seem as if the ghost of the "real Republic" had all but vanished but a guerrilla campaign in the border area flared between 1956 and 1962. This campaign was dealt with by the governments in the North and the South according to a pattern that was now well established: internment, some censorship, and special judicial procedures. Once again, by the late 1960s the IRA appeared to be totally shattered. North-South relations had rarely been as amicable and, consequently, partition had ceased to be a burning issue.

1968 ushered in a totally new chapter in the history of the IRA—a chapter which is still far from closed. The civil rights campaign in Northern Ireland, which started peacefully enough, provoked stern loyalist reactions; and the more the Army sought to keep the peace, the more the initial goodwill of Catholics evaporated with the result that the

IRA found itself cast in the role of defender of the Catholic ghettoes. On February 6, 1971 the first British soldier was killed by an IRA sniper; and bombings became a part of everyday life. Describing the variety of bombs that terrorists can use, Clutterbuck covers the whole spectrum of the IRA bombing campaign:

> The terrorist bomb may be posted in a letter or a parcel; it may be put in a shopping bag, with a time fuse, in a pub, a bus-station or a tourist centre like the Tower of London, and be left to blow up indiscriminately whoever may be there. It may be left in a suitcase or carton in a station baggage room, in the baggage compartment of a public building. It may be locked in the boot of a car; or it may simply be a booby trap to be set off by any simple action, such as opening a door or treading on a floorboard.[9]

On July 21, 1972, 22 bombs exploded in Belfast, killing nine people, and injuring over a hundred. In August 1976, the British ambassador in Dublin was killed when a land mine blew up his car; and a similar bomb killed four RUC men near Bessbrook in early 1979. In August 1979, Lord Mountbatten was killed when his yacht was blown up off the coast of County Sligo. Besides bombs, snipers have taken a steady toll of soldiers, policemen, and civilians. But by no means all the killing has been done by the PIRA. In January 1972 British paratroopers killed thirteen men in Derry and, in early 1978, a number of men were shot dead at Ballysillan Post Office while in the process of planting bombs. Moreover, there have been numerous assassinations both between and within the two communities in Northern Ireland, not least among the various Loyalist paramilitary groups.

The position of the Republic's government has been difficult throughout this latest PIRA campaign since the killings have been largely confined to Northern Ireland. Although the Irish government was obviously concerned with the plight of Catholics in the North, there was little direct help that could be given to "our people." This feeling of frustration was most intense in the wake of the deaths of the thirteen civilians shot dead in Londonderry in January 1972. For many people in the South, the IRA had the same concern as the government for the welfare of the Catholic ghettoes but whereas the government could only make vain promises ("we will not stand idly by") the IRA was seen to be doing something on the ground. It was not difficult for Cabinet

Ministers in the South to applaud secretly the defensive role of the IRA in the North while publicly condemning violence. The apparent ambivalence of the Irish government has stemmed largely from a sense of helplessness at not being able to influence events in an area where they have no jurisdiction. C. C. O'Brien has captured this mood:

> Mr. Lynch condemned violence, indeed he did. He also said that ''violence is a by-product of the division of the country''. This seemed to imply that violence would go on as long as partition did, and that those who were responsible for the violence, which Mr. Lynch so unfailingly condemned, were those who maintained that partition. Did this imply that the IRA, though a little hot-headed, perhaps, were by and large right?[10]

A similar ambivalence runs through Irish attitudes toward the IRA. Many more people are prepared to tolerate the IRA than actively support it although few would say so publicly. In parts of rural Ireland, it makes people ''feel good'' to have an IRA man living in the neighborhood, and they will do good turns for him even though they publicly disown his methods, and even his aims. This rather schizophrenic attitude toward the IRA stems largely from the complex concatenation of ideas which constitute Republican ''ideology.''

## The Ideology

''Ideology'' may be a rather grandiose term to ascribe to the network of tactics and goals which underlie PIRA's campaign at the present time. Not only are short-term aims and long-term goals difficult to distinguish, but Republicanism, like any nationalist ideology, weaves together divergent threads of argument into a messy tapestry. The *leitmotiv* running through all Republican thought is hostility to the presence of British influence, in any shape or form, in Ireland. But, beyond that, there has been continual disagreement as to how the British presence should be faced. The internal feuding that is endemic in the Republican movement revolves around ''collaborative'' and ''triumphalist'' strategies—a dichotomy which has now hardened into the split between OIRA and PIRA. But this is merely the latest fission: there is no doubt that the ''republican'' strategy of Irish governments, particularly under De Valera, went a long way toward siphoning off much support for the IRA with the result that the great mass of the population is content with "half a loaf."

The resilience of the IRA as a viable movement has puzzled and fascinated observers. There can be few movements in Europe which have shown such powers of survival for over half a century. This is not easy to explain but one reason for it must be the variety of ideological currents which have been subsumed under the Republican banner. Like a typical "nationalist" movement, Republicanism has managed to attract adherents from a wide social spectrum—soldiers, scholars, workers—and to include (although uneasily) fascist and socialist tendencies within its ranks.

The major split between OIRA and PIRA is sometimes rather superficially classified as a split between the Right and the Left but this is something of an oversimplification. The PIRA advocacy of "national liberation" before "national socialism" is diametrically opposed to the OIRA strategy of winning over working-class support in both the Republic and the North before pushing for unification.

But, for the moment, the initiative belongs to PIRA, and the British presence in Northern Ireland is the *casus belli*. Not because the British presence is a new development but because of the implications of that presence, PIRA believes that it has a mission to free the Catholic working population from the "injustices" that Britain has done nothing to mitigate. In other words, the aspirations awakened by the civil rights movement presented the IRA with a new opportunity after a period in the doldrums. As Bowyer Bell puts it:

> By 1962 many others had long since faded away in despair, in disgrace or in dudgeon. The Army was a husk—its strength eroded, its purpose lost, its future unclear.[11]

The rejuvenation of the IRA, in its Provisional guise, from 1969 onward can be directly related to the experiences of the Catholic population in the North. PIRA argued that they were needed as the defenders of the Catholic population against British Army incursions and Loyalist gunmen. It is clear that support for PIRA in areas like Ballymurphy and Turf Lodge has fluctuated according to perceptions of how the security forces have acted in those areas. To "lift" suspects, the Army had to conduct searches, and "screen" civilians over a wide area. Inevitably, such searches could often be humiliating, distasteful, violent, or abusive although not necessarily so. To some of the people living in these areas, it was sometimes difficult to distinguish between the "lawlessness" of the IRA and the "lawlessness" of soldiers who, under vague and sweeping legislation, could act as policeman, judge, and executioner, all in one. A "participant-observer" in a Belfast Catholic ghetto writes:

> Soldiers not only apprehend and detain suspects, they beat them. They interrogate with illegal methods ranging from ill-treatment to torture. They wreak vengeance for their dead comrades.[12]

Against a background of harassment in the Catholic areas, PIRA was able to argue that the short-term crisis could best be resolved by ending partition since it could only be in a united Ireland that justice for the Catholic population could be achieved. As for their offensive operations in the rural areas of Northern Ireland, PIRA has argued that these are the best way to distract the Army's attention from the Catholic ghettoes. As a bonus, such guerrilla operations might hasten the day when the British would decide to leave Ireland for good simply because it had become too costly to stay.

Support for PIRA tends to be stronger in the Catholic areas when it confines itself to defensive operations. The offensive role is much more controversial since it invites retaliation and repression in the very areas which PIRA purports to protect. Indeed, it is sometimes argued that PIRA generates the conditions which are used to justify its continuing campaign.

A major focus of allegiance among Catholics is the Church. One indication of the strength of this allegiance is the effort made by PIRA to reconcile its own activities with the doctrines of the Church. Traditionally, of course, the Roman Catholic hierarchy has given short shrift in public to the IRA. The local priests deprecate the violence of PIRA without condemning their long-term goal. The PIRA response to intrusions from the Church is either to argue that political and religious matters should be kept separate (i.e., that priests should mind their own business) or to justify their campaign in quasi-religious terms. Thus:

> The Provisionals argue they can be good Catholics by appealing to the ultimate sanctity of the conscience. They strive to make a distinction be-

tween religious and political dogma and they reserve the right to use violence in a just war.[13]

The Catholic Church has generally taken the line that government security forces should be supported provided they behave within the law. Thus, while many priests privately aspire to a 32-county Ireland, they do not condone the use of violence to achieve it. However, the Church has been careful not to alienate its own supporters by turning a blind eye to a more insidious form of violence—that practiced by the state. In 1971, the Catholic bishops in Northern Ireland condemned, in a joint statement, all violence as being "contrary to the law of Christ" and alluded to "some particularly cold-blooded murders in recent weeks." They then went on to condemn

> another form of violence which is also shameful and contrary to the law of Christ. We refer to the process known as "interrogation in depth" as it has been practised in Northern Ireland in recent months. Men have been kept hooded and standing, with arms and legs outstretched. . . . These were men who had been imprisoned without trial. . . . The solution to our present tragic situation will never be found in violence or counter-violence.[14]

The PIRA campaign in Northern Ireland is based on the supposition that a substantial part of the Catholic working class lives in a state of chronic "oppression" by virtue of living in a 6-county unit where British force underwrites a sectarian hegemony. Popular support for PIRA wavers according to how British rule is perceived. At times when Britain appears to fall short of its own standards of justice, PIRA can expect greater support. This is particularly the case when allegations of brutality against the security forces are either ignored by the authorities or "whitewashed" by an official inquiry. (The use of judges as chairmen for these official inquiries, which is intended to remove the investigations from the political arena, serves only to taint the judicial system with political bias.)

The fact that PIRA displays such resilience in the face of the forces ranged against it is explained by the reservoir of passive support that PIRA enjoys. The image of a small band of ruthless criminals holding a cowering population to ransom is a comforting illusion but it has little to do with reality. A purely military victory over PIRA is not possible in the context of a liberal democratic society. No one realizes this more clearly than the soldiers who are engaged in this frustrating task. The battle is a battle for legitimacy and, therefore, it is all the more important that the state should employ methods which are in its own best traditions and which conform to its own ideological goals. Time and time again the "security" approach to defeating PIRA has only furnished it with new recruits. The key to the elimination of violence lies in creating a political atmosphere where PIRA would simply be irrelevant, where tacit support for PIRA would be transformed into outright rejection.

One is often asked what sort of Ireland PIRA is fighting for. The ordinary member of an Active Service Unit is not politically sophisticated. He may believe he is fighting for the end of British rule in Ireland, or for a "32-county Republic" but, beyond that, the political planning has been left to Provisional Sinn Fein (PSF), which is the political wing of PIRA and is not a proscribed organization either in the Republic or in Northern Ireland. From the point of view of the state, the existence of PSF is important since it allows for some sort of communication with PIRA without too much political embarrassment. PSF and PIRA view themselves as the "civil" and "military" wings, respectively, of the Republican movement in which they play equal and complementary roles. In fact, the major decisions relating to military and political matters tend to be taken by the Army Council (within PIRA).

Eire Nua, or the "New Ireland" envisaged by PSF would be based on a federation of the four historic provinces—Ulster, Connacht, Leinster, and Munster. The federal capital would be located in Athlone but substantial powers would be reserved to the four provincial parliaments of which one, Dail Uladh (the Parliament of Ulster), would have a Protestant majority. Below the provincial level, power would be further delegated to regions and below them to the "pobol" (district councils for communities of 10,000–40,000 people). Thus Eire Nua would be "a community of communities." The economic aspects of the New Ireland would also be fundamentally different: the nationalization of key industries; the severing of foreign control; departure from the EEC; and the greater exploitation of Ireland's "natural resources." Culturally, the Irish language would become predominant. In foreign affairs links would be forged with the third world.

The whole complexion of this political and economic program is a studied repudiation of the major influences on the Irish economy and political system in the twentieth century. The economic program rejects the "modernizing" forces of foreign investment which have tied Ireland so closely to Britain and to Europe. The political program rejects the high degree of centralization which characterized British rule before partition and subsequent governments in both parts of Ireland.

In the meantime, however, PSF has two main concerns: to end British rule in Ireland, and to secure an amnesty for all political prisoners. Prisoners have always played an important part in Republican tradition. The escapes, the hunger strikes, the martyrdoms—these have been recurring events which are every bit as important as the achievements on "active service." The idea that laws and justice go together has not been readily apparent to IRA men. The law itself has often been tarnished by the actions of "overzealous" servants of the state: the Black and Tans, the RIC, the B-Specials, the Paras. Historical memories are continually revived by modern analogies. Burton cites an example from present-day Belfast:

> There are memories like those of old Mrs. Johnson who told me how, as a young girl she had seen a man abducted by the Black and Tans. He was found dead later on in the day. Mrs. Johnson sees the British troops of today in the very same street as latter-day Tans.[15]

Part of the explanation for the long survival of the IRA lies exactly in this repetitiveness—the fact that contemporary events so often evoke vivid and bitter memories which, in themselves, are enough to stiffen resistance and exclude compromise.

This obduracy is very apparent in the current H-block protest.[16] This protest lies at the center of PIRA concerns at the moment for two reasons. Firstly, it challenges the state's view that the PIRA campaign is not "politically motivated." Secondly, it is linked in the Republican mind with a string of prison protests stretching back to the 1920s. The release of the first H-block protester, Kieran Nugent, in May 1979 gave the press a chance to hear, at first hand, what the protest involved. Of Kieran Nugent himself, the *Irish Times* wrote:

> His background helps to explain the stubborn courage of the H-block prisoners. He comes from a family of 10 in the Lower Falls, Belfast. After a decade of war and generations of neglect this ghetto has become a wasteland. Its

people have always known repression and for them a united Ireland represents the prospect of a fair chance in life.[17]

and of the protest in general:

> How do they endure these conditions? "Mind over body" was the clichéd expression. Shared privation has created a sense of solidarity among these tough working class men; they are strengthened by the ministry of their church and by the devotion of relatives and friends. . . .[18]

The H-block protest is probably the most burning issue of contention between the state and PIRA at the present time. Its symbolic value outweighs its material implications both to the protesters and to the government. The government is just as unwilling to reverse its view that "convicted criminals must be treated as criminals" as PIRA is to accept the view that they are criminals.

## The Response of the State

The division of the island of Ireland into two political units is not only a major grievance for PIRA, it is also one of the main obstacles to a successful pursuit of PIRA by the two states concerned. During the sixty years of partition, the activities of the IRA have rarely had a uniform impact in both North and South, and neither the perceptions of the IRA nor the strategies used to tackle IRA violence have been similar.

In the period since 1969, it has been Northern Ireland which has borne the brunt of PIRA's campaign. The existence of two jurisdictions in Ireland has meant that PIRA has been able to elude security forces in the North by disappearing south of the border. This has led opinion in the North to regard towns like Dundalk and Castleblayney as "bases" from which PIRA has been able to launch incursions into the North. No amount of cross-border cooperation can replace the "right of hot pursuit"; and it is undoubtedly a considerable frustration to the British Army in the North that, whereas the great mass of the population (including terrorists) can cross the border quite freely, it (i.e., the Army) must observe the territorial limits of the Republic most scrupulously.

In the legal sphere, there has been antiterrorist legislation on the books in both the Republic and Northern Ireland virtually without a break since 1920. Despite the fact that British governments (and Northern Ireland politicians) accuse the South of being a "haven for terrorists," "soft on the IRA" and so on, the antiterrorist legislation in the Republic is probably a greater invasion of civil liberties than is tolerated in any other Western liberal democracy at the present time. In one respect, at least, PIRA was much worse off in the Republic up to 1974 than it was in the United Kingdom in that it was a proscribed organization in the former and, since 1976, the IRA has been denied all publicity through the media—something which is not yet the case in the United Kingdom.

The Republic's main judicial response to subversive organizations like the IRA has been the Offences Against the State Act (1939) which has been amended on more than one occasion since to take account of the current PIRA campaign. In 1972, Part V of the Act was invoked to establish the Special Criminal Court. This consists of an uneven number of judges (usually three) and no jury. The Court is intended to deal with cases where a threat to the state is involved, and where there is reason to believe that a normal jury trial would not suffice. Except for the lack of a jury, the Court's procedure is supposed to follow that of a normal court. Even so, the Court did not succeed in securing many convictions against PIRA until the end of 1972 when the Dail passed another Amendment which made it easier to secure such convictions. This Amendment placed the onus on an individual to repudiate any published allegation that he was a member of the IRA; and the failure to do so would be taken as evidence of such membership.[19] Moreover, a statement by a senior Garda officer that a person is a member of the IRA would henceforward be taken as evidence of such membership.[20] The burden of proof, once again, fell on the individual to disprove his membership of an illegal organization. In this respect, the Republic's legislation is more stringent than similar legislation in Northern Ireland. In yet another Amendment to the Act in 1976, in the wake of the killing of the British ambassador in Dublin, spokesmen for illegal organizations were not allowed to appear on radio or television, or be quoted in the press. Again, the contrast with British legislation can be noted, since the interview with an Irish National Liberation Army (INLA) representative (the group who claim Airey Neave's death) on BBC television in mid-1979 would have been illegal in the Republic (but note, also, that most viewers in the Republic can pick up BBC television programs).

Needless to say, the rather draconian provisions of the Offences Against the State Act, and its several amendments, have given rise to some concern in the Republic that the normal judicial process, with its protection for the accused, has been seriously jeopardized. This feeling has been exacerbated by the fact that the Special Criminal Court has been used for cases which were not obviously "political" in nature,[21] although the distinction between "political" and "nonpolitical" offences is not one which this Act recognizes.

The other piece of legislation worthy of mention is the Criminal Law Jurisdiction Act (1975) which is designed to extend the criminal law to cover crimes committed in Northern Ireland and Britain. A procedure is established whereby a court can obtain evidence from witnesses too frightened to travel for the purpose. A reciprocal Act has been passed in Britain (The Criminal Jurisdiction Act) which makes complementary provisions. This pair of Acts constitutes a rudimentary foundation for the kind of comprehensive legal cooperation which will be needed throughout the British Isles if the full weight of the law is to be felt by any illegal organizations like the PIRA. Even this modest beginning had a difficult passage through the Dail although its enactment was greatly accelerated by bomb explosions in Dublin streets. The major stumbling block still remaining is the refusal of the Republic to extradite suspects to the United Kingdom for offences which can be regarded as "political." The Irish Constitution is cited as the reason for this refusal.[22]

In Northern Ireland, the principal antiterrorist legislation was the Special Powers Act (1922) which was replaced by the Emergency Provisions Act in 1973. This Act has been amended from time to time since 1973 and the latest consolidated Act dates from 1978. By far the most controversial aspect of emergency legislation has been the power to imprison without trial. In 1975, detention without trial was considerably modified. The power became vested in the Secretary of State to make "interim custody orders" which were subject to review. The numbers of people detained under the new procedure gradually diminished. It is widely agreed that mass detention without trial proved to be counterproductive since so many innocent people became enmeshed in the process, and consequently disaffected from the judicial system. The fact that detention operated so much more against Catholics than Protestants did nothing to win "hearts and minds" in the minority community to support the forces of law and order.

Another aspect of the emergency legislation has been the suspension of trial by jury. The argument here is that in a society where juries were being constantly challenged and intimidated, the normal process of law cannot operate. The so-called "Diplock courts" have undoubtedly streamlined the judicial process; and there have been no serious allegations of bias in their operation. The Gardiner Committee, reporting in 1975, concluded that, although a return to jury trials should be achieved as soon as conditions permitted, the Diplock System was not, in itself, a major source of grievance.[23] Nevertheless, public opinion in Northern Ireland remains in favor of a return to trial by jury.

Other aspects of emergency legislation include arrest without a warrant; prolonged periods of holding suspects without charges being brought; and special powers for the police to search. The Prevention of Terrorism Act (1974), which was passed in England but applies to England and Northern Ireland, increased police powers against terrorist suspects. This Act, which was passed in the aftermath of the Birmingham bombs (November 1974) when twenty civilians died, proscribed the IRA. The most controversial aspects of this Act, however, have been the powers to exclude any person from Britain who is suspected of being a terrorist.[24] Even people resident in Britain for up to twenty years can be expelled across the Irish Sea to either Northern Ireland or the Republic. The Act also empowers police at ports to detain people for questioning if they think they may have some useful information. The maximum period for such interrogation is seven days (with the Home Secretary's approval). From 1974 to June 1979, 4,146 persons were thus detained for questioning—mainly at Liverpool and Heathrow Airport. Under "exclusion orders," in the same period, 140 people were removed from Britain to Northern Ireland, and 29 to the Republic. About 90 percent of the people detained at ports had no charges brought against them. A recent report from the National Council for Civil Liberties says that the Act "nullifies the remedy of a writ of habeas corpus, by making it lawful for the police to arrest on extremely wide grounds"; and it also claims that fingerprint records and photos of all those questioned are kept in police files.[25]

## Survey Evidence

We now turn to consider some survey evidence which lends strength to the supposition that the PIRA can draw on a pool of, at least, passive support in its activities although the extent of this support is likely to fluctuate under the pressure of specific circumstances. It is argued here, in other words, that if the guerrilla "fish" need water to survive, then adequate water exists.

Much of the attitudinal information presented here is drawn from the Northern Ireland Attitude Survey which was carried out under the author's supervision in the fall of 1978. The number of respondents involved was 1,277, selected on the basis of a stratified random sample, and was, on the basis of ensuing tests, reasonably representative of the Northern Ireland population as a whole. The other main source of attitudinal information used here is the parallel survey carried out simultaneously in the Irish Republic by Davis and Sinnott.[26] Their respondents numbered 1,758 and the use of several matching items in the two surveys allows North-South comparisons to be made. Both surveys gathered information on a wide range of topics including "national identity," "party affiliations," "religiosity," attitudes toward various scenarios involving Northern Ireland and, of most concern to us here, perceptions of the paramilitary groups as well as the response of the state to them. We will also consider one or two other opinion polls where the findings are relevant to the subject in hand.

In the following analysis, potential or passive support for the PIRA is examined from three distinct perspectives. Firstly, we consider reactions of respondents to items which actually contain a reference to the IRA. Second, we will compare reactions of respondents in Northern Ireland with those in the Republic toward measures being taken by the state against the IRA. Thirdly, we estimate the extent to which the avowed aims and concerns of the PIRA are consonant with aspirations in the broader community. The intention here is not to suggest that sharing the aims of the PIRA is to be actively supportive of them, but rather to underline that the PIRA often operates in a politically sympathetic atmosphere. In this respect, if no other, PIRA can be distinguished from other groups which are labeled "terrorist," such as the Brigate Rosse and the Baader-Meinhof gang, and possibly has more in common with the Sandinistas in Nicaragua and the former guerrillas of Zimbabwe.

In Table 1, three Likert[27] items referring directly to the IRA provoke particularly strong reactions among Protestant respondents. Note also that, in each case, Catholics are less likely to dismiss the IRA as being totally peripheral to the situation in Northern Ireland. The 34.2 percent of Catholics who disagree that the IRA are just "criminals and murder-

**TABLE 1**
**Attitudes Toward the IRA in Northern Ireland**

"Were it not for the IRA, the Northern Ireland problem would be even further from a solution"

|  | Catholics % | Protestants % |
|---|---|---|
| Strongly disagree | 28.5 | 61.1 |
| Moderately disagree | 25.4 | 18.3 |
| Slightly disagree | 13.5 | 9.0 |
| Slightly agree | 14.1 | 4.1 |
| Moderately agree | 10.7 | 3.0 |
| Strongly agree | 7.9 | 4.4 |

"The IRA are basically patriots and idealists"

|  | Catholics % | Protestants % |
|---|---|---|
| Strongly disagree | 18.8 | 45.8 |
| Moderately disagree | 19.9 | 13.0 |
| Slightly disagree | 14.9 | 6.5 |
| Slightly agree | 21.8 | 11.6 |
| Moderately agree | 15.7 | 9.2 |
| Strongly agree | 8.8 | 13.9 |

"The IRA are basically a bunch of criminals and murderers"

|  | Catholics % | Protestants % |
|---|---|---|
| Strongly disagree | 11.8 | 2.1 |
| Moderately disagree | 9.6 | 1.9 |
| Slightly disagree | 12.9 | 3.8 |
| Slightly agree | 21.2 | 5.0 |
| Moderately agree | 21.2 | 13.0 |
| Strongly agree | 23.4 | 74.2 |

*Source:* Northern Ireland Attitude Survey.     N = 1277

ers" presumably attribute some ulterior motives to their campaign. This hypothesis is strengthened by the fact that 46.3 percent of Catholics attribute motives of "patriotism and idealism" to the IRA—an attitude which is shared by about a third of the Protestants in the sample. If the problem in Northern Ireland can be defined as political, then the 32 percent of Catholics who feel that the IRA has, in some way, acted as a catalyst (if only by delineating the issues more clearly) in the situation, are according the group some political significance.

From what has been said, it follows that a substantial minority of Protestants regard the IRA as being engaged in a violent campaign which is inspired by something more than "mindless murder." In other words, there is a feeling among some Protestants that while they do not sympathize with the aims of the PIRA or even its methods, they can understand why such methods are being used. The extent to which some Protestant opinion can accept violence as an acceptable method to achieve political ends, can be surmised from Table 2. Here, nearly half the Protestant respondents support the reactions of Loyalist paramilitary organizations. A better way to assess the Protestant reaction to IRA violence is to hypothesize a situation where the Protestant community found itself in a position analogous to that of the Catholic community in Northern Ireland today (i.e., as a minority). In such a situation, a majority of Protestants (63 percent) agree that Loyalist paramilitaries

**TABLE 2**
**Attitudes Toward Loyalist Paramilitary Organizations**
**in Northern Ireland**

"The actions of loyalist paramilitaries are a justified reaction to what has happened in Northern Ireland"

|                     | *Catholics* % | *Protestants* % |
| ------------------- | --------- | ----------- |
| Strongly disagree   | 35.7      | 24.7        |
| Moderately disagree | 27.3      | 18.2        |
| Slightly disagree   | 12.1      | 13.2        |
| Slightly agree      | 12.6      | 20.2        |
| Moderately agree    | 7.0       | 12.4        |
| Strongly agree      | 5.4       | 11.3        |

"If Ireland were ever united, the loyalist paramilitaries would be more of a problem than the IRA is today"

|                     | *Catholics* % | *Protestants* % |
| ------------------- | --------- | ----------- |
| Strongly disagree   | 13.8      | 11.5        |
| Moderately disagree | 20.5      | 13.9        |
| Slightly disagree   | 13.2      | 11.5        |
| Slightly agree      | 13.2      | 16.0        |
| Moderately agree    | 21.6      | 19.1        |
| Strongly agree      | 17.6      | 28.0        |

*Source:* Northern Ireland Attitude Survey.      N = 1277

would constitute a greater challenge to the status quo than the IRA does in Northern Ireland today. The conclusion is clear. Given a political situation in which a minority feels threatened, force is one of the methods by which that threat will be faced. Such a conclusion is reinforced by Rose's 1968 survey[28] which found that 82 percent of Protestants agreed that it was right for people (50 years previously) to "take up arms and stand ready to fight to keep Northern Ireland British";[29] and 52 percent of Protestants agreed that "today it would be right to take any measures necessary in order to keep Northern Ireland a Protestant country."[30] On the Catholic side, Rose found that 60 percent agreed that (50 years previously) it had been right for people "to take up arms and fight in order to make the Republic."[31]

We now turn to consider the amount of support that is forthcoming for measures which are either being taken or could be taken by the state against the IRA. Here we will be concerned with public opinion on both sides of the Irish border since this border, besides being a central issue in the PIRA campaign, constitutes a serious obstacle to effective state responses in the judicial and military spheres. In Table 3, a number of Likert items allow comparisons to be made not only between Catholics and Protestants in Northern Ireland but also between both communities and opinion in the Republic. Several inferences can be drawn from these comparisons. Firstly, Protestant opinion in the North is overwhelmingly in favor of stronger governmental measures against the IRA. Such a feeling applies equally to the Irish and British governments. On the other hand, Catholic opinion in the North is much more ambivalent, as is also opinion in the Republic generally. This suggests either that tighter security may infringe on civil liberties to a degree which is regarded as excessive or, more plausibly, that doubts are being expressed about the implied assumption that blame can be laid exclusively at the door of the PIRA. In this context, it is worth noting that Catholic opinion in Northern Ireland is more inclined to support tougher governmental measures than is opinion in the Republic. This can be explained, presumably, by the fact that Catholic opinion in the North is more familiar with, and more supportive of, British rule than is the case in the Republic. Secondly, efforts to combat the cross-border dimension of PIRA violence are strongly endorsed by Protestant opinion (9 out of 10 respondents believing that the Irish government is not doing enough to restrain the PIRA incursions), but Catholic opinion in the North is

**TABLE 3**
**Attitudes Toward Measures Against the IRA in Northern Ireland and in the Republic of Ireland**

|  | Northern Ireland | | Republic |
|  | Cath. | Prot. |  |
|  | % | % | % |
| "The British Government should take a tougher line with the IRA" *Agree* | 55 | 94 | 46 |
| "The Irish Government should take a tougher line with the IRA" *Agree* | 64 | 97 | 63 |
| "The Irish Government is not doing its best to ensure that the IRA is unable to operate from the Republic's side of the Border" *Agree* | 41 | 91 | 45 |
| "The Irish Government should agree to extradition, that is, to agree to hand over to the authorities in Northern Ireland or Britain, people accused of politically motivated crimes there" *Agree* | 67 | 98 | 46 |

*Source:* ESRI Survey (for the Republic) and the Northern Ireland Attitude Survey for Nothern Ireland. N (Republic) = 1758. N (Northern Ireland) = 1277.

N.B. In this table, percentages are rounded to nearest whole digit. The % agreeing is the total of those agreeing either "slightly," "moderately," or "strongly."

divided on this, as are respondents in the Republic. This contrast in attitudes between Catholics and Protestants is reflected in the extent of support there is for extradition of terrorist suspects—a measure which would undoubtedly curb cross-border activity. On this issue, Protestants feel extremely strongly (98 percent supporting extradition; see Table 3). However, there is almost as much difference of opinion between Northern Catholics and their coreligionists in the Republic as there is between them and the Northern Protestants. The reluctance of the Irish government to extradite terrorist suspects to the North may be justifiable in the light of public opinion, which is clearly divided on the issue. This ambivalence may be attributable to Constitutional[32] inhibitions (which are often offered as the explanation) or it may be due to a feeling that the due process of law is adequate in the Republic in view of the antiterrorist laws that have been enacted there during the past decade.[33] This latter sentiment may be coupled, in some cases, with a feeling that a suspect may not get a fair trial in the North. However, the problems in operating the Criminal Law Jurisdiction Act,[34] and the rather more tolerant attitude displayed toward the IRA in the Republic, mean that the border still represents, to some extent, a ''shield'' behind which the fugitive can shelter.

The suggestion that public opinion in the Republic is more tolerant of the IRA than opinion in the North needs to be explored further since, if such a suggestion is substantiated, it would explain why there is less enthusiasm in the South for more stringent measures against the IRA. The Davis and Sinnott survey (from which data on the Republic have been taken) concluded that there is more support for the IRA than is commonly assumed. By factor-analyzing a number of Likert items they arrived at a measure of support for the ''motives'' of the IRA (42 percent) and another for the ''activities'' of the IRA (21 percent).[35] Both figures, when published, were greeted with a certain amount of incredulity by both politicians and the press.[36] However, Davis and Sinnott had entered a note of caution:

> In regard to the remaining 21% support for IRA activities, it should first of all be noted that this includes 13% who are slightly supportive as against 8% moderately to strongly supportive. This having been said, the stark fact remains that 21% of the population emerge as in some degree supportive in their attitude to IRA activities.[37]

Support for IRA activities which includes, of course, support for the use of violence, may be an essential ingredient in the Irish political culture. In a survey carried out in 1972 among Irish secondary school children,[38] it was found that, although a majority deplored the use of violence generally, and the actions of the IRA specifically, there was a not insignificant minority who felt that the IRA was doing ''what is necessary'' in Northern Ireland (29.6 percent); and 40 percent were prepared to condone the use of force by the Irish government to end British rule in Northern Ireland.[39] The authors of this survey report could not avoid the conclusion that, among Irish adolescents, there was a feeling that although violence was regrettable, it was justifiable in circumstances where there was no alternative way of bringing about a more desirable state of affairs. Here it is worth noting that the Irish Republic owes its origins to a bloody "war of independence" and that Irish political culture would find it natural to justify violence in pursuit of desirable political goals.

Finally, we consider the extent to which there is popular support for the goals which the PIRA claims to be fighting for, or concern about issues which they claim to be legitimate grievances. Taking first the central tenet of Republican ideology—the existence of a partitioned island—the Northern Ireland Attitude Survey found that 71.4 percent of Catholics agreed with the suggestion that there "will never be peace in Ireland until partition is ended." On the complementary but more specific question of a British withdrawal from Northern Ireland, Catholic opinion is extremely ambivalent, a possible implication being that the circumstances in which such a withdrawal would take place would be a prime consideration. In the same survey, Catholic respondents were divided half and half on the question of whether the British government "should announce its intention to withdraw whether the majority agrees or not."[40] The term "British withdrawal" is a trifle vague since it could refer to several different manifestations of the British presence (and for Protestants the notion is further complicated by the fact that most of them regard themselves as "British"). When the question is limited to the "British Army," an ITN poll (taken in May 1979) found that 91 percent of Protestants and 47 percent of Catholics felt that it would be "in the best interests of Northern Ireland" for the Army to remain. The consequences of a British Army withdrawal were widely regarded as undesirable (see Table 4).

Attitudes toward different branches of the security forces within Northern Ireland reveal, unsurprisingly, a gap between Catholic and Protestant levels of approval. In Table 5 it can be seen that whereas Protestants make virtually no distinction between the Royal Ulster Constabulary (RUC), the Ulster Defence Regiment (UDR), and the British Army, Catholics make a distinction between the RUC and the British Army, on the one hand, and the UDR on the other. This suggests that two hypotheses can be set on one side. One is that locally recruited forces would prove more acceptable to Catholics than the exogenous British Army. The other is that the outside force (i.e., the Army) might prove more acceptable since it could be considered more impartial. The fact that the UDR is rated lower than the Army and the RUC by Catholics may be accounted for by the higher proportion of Catholics

## TABLE 4
### Attitudes in Northern Ireland Toward "British Withdrawal"

"There will never be peace in Ireland until partition is ended"

|  | Catholics % | Protestants % |
|---|---|---|
| Agree | 71 | 36 |

"The British Government should declare their intention to withdraw whether the majority in Northern Ireland agrees or not"

|  | Catholics % | Protestants % |
|---|---|---|
| Agree | 50 | 12 |

*Source:* Northern Ireland Attitude Survey.        N = 1277

"If the British Government were to withdraw troops from the North without a political solution having been achieved, what would the most likely consequence be?"

|  | Catholics % | Protestants % |
|---|---|---|
| Civil war involving the whole of Ireland | 27 | 46 |
| Complete breakdown in law and order | 28 | 39 |
| An independent Northern Ireland with a government containing representatives of both communities | 16 | 6 |
| A United Ireland with order kept by the Irish Army | 9 | 1 |
| An independent Northern Ireland with a Unionist Government | 2 | 4 |
| Don't know | 18 | 4 |

*Source:* ITN poll (July 1979)        N = 632

serving in the RUC but that, of course, is only a partial explanation since one would need to account for the relatively stronger Catholic recruitment into the RUC.

The need for the RUC to gain acceptability among all sections of the population has been rendered more urgent in the context of current government policy which is to control terrorism through the "due process of the law." Such a policy has, as its central feature, the "primacy of the police." Allegations that the RUC had used excessive force when questioning suspects at certain interrogation centers led to an Amnesty International investigation[41] whose findings resulted in the

**TABLE 5**
**Attitudes Toward the Security Forces in Northern Ireland**

|  |  | *Catholics* *%* | *Protestants* *%* |
|---|---|---|---|
| "The RUC is doing its job well" | *Agree* | 73 | 94 |
| "The UDR is doing its job well" | *Agree* | 64 | 94 |
| "The British Army is doing its job well" | *Agree* | 71 | 92 |
| "Stories about the RUC beating people up in custody are just propaganda" | *Agree* | 22 | 64 |

*Source:* The Northern Ireland Attitude Survey.    N = 1277

setting up of an inquiry[42] under Judge Bennett in the fall of 1978. As long as the public believes that those who are the agents of the law sometimes stray beyond it, the opponents of the state will be able to erode its legitimacy. In the Northern Ireland Attitude Survey 64 percent of Protestants and 22 percent of Catholics agreed with the suggestion that "stories of the RUC beating people up in custody are just propaganda." Whatever the facts of the matter, the conclusions of the Amnesty International investigation were clearly reflected in widespread public concern,[43] especially among Catholics. In a judicial system where not only the substance but also the appearance of legality are emphasized, there is little room for complacency.

As suggested earlier,[44] the challenge to the state's legitimacy is nowhere more acute than in the current campaign for "political status" among prisoners in Northern Ireland. The fact that there appears to be some support among the public for the position being taken by these prisoners will make it more, rather than less, difficult for either side to abandon its entrenched attitude. In Table 6, data from the Republic of Ireland and Northern Ireland summarize the extent to which the prisoners' campaign finds an echo of sympathy outside. The support among Protestants for such political status must be seen in the context of what was said earlier[45] about the Loyalist "understanding" of the PIRA campaign despite the lack of sympathy for it. And, of course, there are a number of Loyalist prisoners who also seek some kind of special status. The data in Table 6 also complement our earlier finding that 34.2 percent of Catholics disagree that the IRA are just "criminals and

**TABLE 6**
**Attitudes Toward "Political Status" in Northern Ireland and the Republic
of Ireland**

| | | Northern Ireland | | Republic |
| | | Prots. | Caths. | |
| | | % | % | % |
| "The British Government should stop treating people convicted of crimes which they claim were politically motivated, as ordinary prisoners" | Agree | 35 | 57 | 60 |

*Source:* The Northern Ireland Attitude Survey (N.I.).    N = 1277
         The ESRI Survey (Republic).                 N = 1758

murderers.'' In other words, they are attributing other motives to the campaign.

In sum, the survey evidence presented here indicates that there is a reservoir of potential support for the aims, if not the activities, of the PIRA. In this respect, the PIRA can be distinguished from other terrorist groups in Western Europe who tend to survive beyond the pale of the societies they threaten. Their activities and movements must, of necessity, be covert, and they must use a greater degree of menace to find refuge among the population. The PIRA, on the other hand, can count on a certain amount of acquiescence, if not acceptance, in the society which spawns it. Its roots run deep into the population on whose grievances it feeds. Its members are not very different from the mass of the Catholic working class.[46] Their ideology is less revolutionary than that of the Baader-Meinhof gang, or the Brigate Rosse, since the former aims to complete a "nationalist" struggle, while the latter are opposed to the whole basis of contemporary society. The aim of the PIRA is, in fact, lent credence by the Constitution[47] of the Irish Republic; and the broad notion of a British disengagement from Ireland is supported by a majority of the people in Ireland, not to mention opinion in Britain itself.[48] The fact that the methods used by the PIRA are deplored by most people, and the fact that the final goal of Eire Nua may be fanciful and impractical, are questions of degree. The crucial point is that the direction of the PIRA campaign is parallel and complementary to the main currents in Irish political culture.

## Conclusions

The foregoing discussion is intended to suggest that the problem of PIRA violence in Northern Ireland is not likely to be solved easily. The problem that faces any liberal democratic government is how far to set aside normal judicial procedures in the fight against terrorism. Here, it is possible to distinguish three "models": the war model, the detention model, and the criminal court model.[49] The war model involves, inter alia, shooting suspected terrorists on sight and meting out harsh and arbitrary punishments to those who shelter them. Such a policy can be effective in certain circumstances, but in Northern Ireland it would be likely to result in many innocent lives being lost, and in greater support for the PIRA. The detention model involves interning terrorist suspects without trial. It also includes the policy of "screening" in a routine fashion large numbers of people. Since both policies involve wholesale suspensions of the normal legal process, there is a risk of further alienating large sections of the community. The criminal court model entails treating terrorists like ordinary criminals. Thus, as far as possible, normal police methods of detection and arrest are employed; and the ensuing trials follow, as closely as possible, the normal pattern. In practice, some aspects of this "normal process" may have to be deleted, but the general advantage of this model is that it minimizes the risk of alienating public opinion and, hence, of aiding recruitment to the PIRA.

Although the third model is now being applied by the state, it is greatly diluted by the extraordinary legislation which has, necessarily, been introduced in stages during the past ten years. On the other hand, the further the judicial system in Northern Ireland becomes removed from norms operating elsewhere in the United Kingdom, the more difficult it is to win support for the state's attempts to maintain law and order. Successive governments have wanted to avoid playing into the hands of PIRA by creating anything resembling a "police state" in that part of the United Kingdom but, at the same time, they have had to avoid giving the impression that a certain level of violence is acceptable[50] provided it does not "spill over" into Britain. Since 1975 the general thrust of security policy has been to treat PIRA acts of violence as ordinary crime and deal with them in the courts. This policy has entailed ignoring any claims that PIRA activities are politically motivated; and it has also entailed giving the police in Northern Ireland the most sophisticated equipment and training for their fight against this sort of "crime."

The Army, as a corollary, has found itself being used increasingly as an armed police force in "support of the civil power" rather than an army proper which could go over to an offensive role. Opinion differs sharply over whether the Army should be allowed a "free hand" to "root out the terrorist" or whether the present restrained profile should be allowed to continue in the interests of avoiding political controversy. From the Army's point of view, the present policy is far from satisfactory as evidenced by the fact that PIRA is still alive and well. The "yellow card" which restricts the circumstances in which a soldier can open fire, means that he must wait for the terrorist to take the initiative.[51] Secondly, the fact that the Army can be used as a police force in areas where the RUC is unacceptable means that soldiers should have the legal powers of policemen in such circumstances.[52] Thirdly, although the Army is supposed to be "aiding the civil power," this civil power in Northern Ireland is sometimes ambivalent, distant, and ill-defined with the result that soldiers sometimes have to act without proper political instructions. Finally, and most crucially, despite public statements to the contrary, the Army knows it cannot succeed in the task it has been assigned. As one officer has remarked, the soldiers sometimes feel that they and the IRA are face to face in the ring while the government acts as referee blowing the whistle when either side oversteps the mark! Since 1972, when the Army was at its most active in Northern Ireland, public opinion has, on balance, been favorable to its presence. But it is also true, as was said earlier, that the excesses of the security forces have been a source of grievance in some of the Catholic ghettoes and a boost for recruitment to PIRA.

The durability of PIRA depends, however, on much more than the conduct of the security forces. The guerrilla fish do have the water they need to survive. The "water" consists of a proportion of the Catholic population which feels that it does not receive a "fair deal" in the Northern Ireland of today. Such a "fair deal" would consist of both tangibles and intangibles, ranging from a notion of "justice" at one extreme to jobs, houses, and leisure amenities, at the other. The role of PIRA has been to capitalize on these perceptions of injustice and link them to a broader struggle. As Burton puts it:

> The IRA has managed to activate from the favourable social struggle of the Catholic communities, a politics of civil rights through national liberation.[53]

As long as this sense of grievance remains, PIRA will be able to find "safe houses." As long as economic and social deprivation persists, as long as the law is enforced in a halfhearted and capricious manner, as long as it seems that some people are above the law, then the battle for legitimacy cannot be won by the state. The attempt to "criminalize" PIRA has not succeeded because, in the battle for legitimacy, it is not enough to hurl insults at your opponents. Legitimacy has to be demonstrated by example.

Support for PIRA is stronger than many observers will care to admit. In a recent editorial, the *Guardian* used the turnout of 7,000 for an IRA demonstration on August 12 to calculate the real measure of support for PIRA:

> If 3 percent support the IRA and another 5 percent give it acquiescence, there are 250,000 people ready to turn a blind eye. . . . Add to those the mass of people in any society who shrug away from involvement in things they do not like and the sea is large enough for many a guerrilla to swim in.[54]

This support could, however, be decimated if the sense of injustice that pervades the ghettoes could be eradicated. This is not to argue that the gun would be put on the shelf overnight or, indeed, ever but that the "sea" in which the "fish" swim would become dangerously shallow.

In sum, I have argued that PIRA is not simply a terrorist movement in the accepted sense of the term. Its longevity, its history, and its goals suggest that it is deeply rooted in the society in which it operates. Although it indulges in acts of terror from time to time, it also fights a military campaign against what it perceives to be an alien army. Unlike the Baader-Meinhof gang, the Brigate Rosse, and other terrorist groups, PIRA's aims are feasible, internally consistent, and find some measure of support among the wider population. In essence, PIRA represents the "cutting edge" of a movement which finds roots in the frustration of relative deprivation experienced by a section of the Catholic community in Northern Ireland.

**Acknowledgments**

The author is indebted to the Committee for Social Science Research in Ireland for its generous support. A shorter version of this article appears as a chapter in J. Lodge (ed.), *Terrorism in the European Community*, London: Martin Robertson (1980).

## Notes

1. P. Wilkinson, *Political Terrorism*, London, Macmillan, 1974, p. 16.
2. Ibid., p. 80.
3. C. C. O'Brien in his *States of Ireland*, London, Panther, 1974, for example, draws on the Maoist analogy of guerrilla "fish" needing the "water" of popular support in order to survive.
4. P. Wilkinson, *Terrorism and the Liberal State*, London, Macmillan, 1977, p. 55.
5. Ibid., p. 56.
6. See, for example, C. Guevara, *Guerrilla Warfare*, Harmondsworth, Penguin, 1969; and R. Debray, *Revolution in the Revolution?* Harmondsworth, Penguin, 1968.
7. For this section, I rely heavily on J. Bowyer Bell, *The Secret Army*, Cambridge, MIT Press, 1970, and by the same author, *A Time of Terror*, New York, Basic Books, 1978, pp. 204–33.
8. J. Bowyer Bell, *A Time of Terror*, p. 209.
9. R. Clutterbuck, *Living with Terrorism*, London, Faber, 1975, pp. 75–76.
10. C. C. O'Brien, op. cit., p. 261.
11. J. Bowyer Bell, *The Secret Army*, p. 337.
12. F. Burton, *The Politics of Legitimacy*, London, RKP, 1978, p. 107.
13. Ibid., p. 104.
14. *Violence in Ireland*, Dublin, Veritas Publications, 1977, pp. 125–26.
15. F. Burton, op. cit., p. 69.
16. Just under four hundred prisoners, mostly Republican but some Loyalist, are refusing to wear prison clothes as part of their campaign to achieve "political status." The protest began on September 14, 1976.
17. *Irish Times*, June 18, 1979.
18. Ibid.
19. Offences Against the State (Amendment) Act 1972, 3(1)b.
20. Ibid., 3(2).
21. M. Robinson, "Special Court Abuses," *Hibernia*, December 6, 1974, and "The Special Criminal Court: Almost Ten Years On," *Fortnight*, No. 175 (March 1980).
22. Specifically Art. 29.3.
23. "Report of a Committee to consider, in the context of civil liberties and human rights, measures to deal with terrorism in Northern Ireland." Cmnd. 5847 (1975), para. 29. See also for a critique of the Diplock courts and other special judicial measures Boyle et al., *Law and State: The Case of Northern Ireland*, London, Martin Robertson, 1975.
24. The Prevention of Terrorism Act (1976), Part II.

25. *Belfast Telegraph,* August 24, 1979.

26. E. Davis and R. Sinnott, *Attitudes in the Republic of Ireland Relevant to the Northern Ireland Problem,* Dublin, ESRI, 1979. Many of the findings of the Northern Ireland Attitude Survey are also reported here.

27. Likert items involve statements put to respondents who are then invited to place themselves on a continuum between e.g., total disagreement and total agreement. See R. Likert, "A Technique for the measurement of attitudes," *Archives of Psychology,* No. 140 (1932).

28. The findings of this survey were published as R. Rose, *Governing Without Consensus,* London, Faber, 1971.

29. Ibid., p. 480.

30. Ibid., p. 480.

31. Ibid., p. 483.

32. Art. 29.3 states that "Ireland accepts the generally recognised principles of international law as its rule of conduct in its relations with other States."

33. 25 percent of those convicted in the Special Criminal Court between 1973 and 1976 were from Northern Ireland. See M. Robinson, "The Special Criminal Court: Almost Ten Years On," *Fortnight,* No. 175 (March 1980).

34. Supra, p. 18.

35. E. Davis and R. Sinnott, op. cit., pp. 94–100.

36. See, for example, "Party leaders reject report on opinions about North" (*Irish Times,* October 17, 1979); "Politicians divided over survey" (*Newsletter,* October 17, 1979); "Lynch rejects '20 p.c. support the IRA' claim," *Irish News,* October 17, 1979.

37. E. Davis and R. Sinnott, op. cit., p. 149.

38. J. Raven et al., *Irish Political Culture: The Views of Two Generations,* Dublin, Institute of Public Administration, 1976.

39. Ibid.

40. E. Davis and R. Sinnott, op. cit., p. 86.

41. *Report of an Amnesty International Mission to Northern Ireland (28 November–6 December 1977),* London, Amnesty International, 1978.

42. The Report of the Committee of Inquiry into Police Interrogation Procedures in Northern Ireland, Cmnd. 7497, HMSO, 1979.

43. The Amnesty International Report had been published shortly before the Northern Ireland Attitude Survey fieldwork commenced.

44. Supra, pp. 14–15.

45. Supra, p. 23.

46. After visiting Republican prisoners in the Maze Prison, Archbishop O'Fiaich said of them: "Many are very youthful and come from families which had never been in trouble with the law, though they lived in areas which suffered discrimination in housing and jobs." From a statement published after the visit on July 30, 1978. See also the secret Army Document No. 37 (dated

February 28, 1978) where it is stated: "PIRA is essentially a working class organization based in the ghetto areas of the cities and in the poorer rural areas." Cited in *Republican News,* May 12, 1979.

47. Art. 2 states that "the national territory consists of the whole island of Ireland, its islands and the territorial seas."

48. For the results of a poll in 1978 in Britain showing that 56 percent of respondents wanted Britain to withdraw from Northern Ireland, and for comparative figures for the Republic and for Northern Ireland, see E. Davis and R. Sinnott, op. cit., p. 86.

49. For a fuller discussion of these three models, see K. Boyle, T. Hadden, and P. Hillyard, "Emergency Powers: Ten Years On," in *Fortnight,* No. 174 (December 1979–January 1980).

50. The phrase "acceptable level of violence" was coined by Mr. Maudling as Home Secretary.

51. P. Wilkinson, *Terrorism and the Liberal State,* p. 157.

52. R. Evelegh, op. cit., passim.

53. F. Burton, op. cit., p. 128.

54. *The Guardian,* August 29, 1979.

# IRA Leadership Problems

## Edgar O'Ballance

*Abstract*     The present leadership of the IRA has been in power for about five years, and appears to be a tight, collective one, with determination to fight a long terrorist campaign until the British government is forced to abandon Northern Ireland. Behind that firm façade are doubts and uncertainties, such as whether the IRA will in fact be able to sustain a long campaign in the face of improved antiterrorist measures. The article traces the development of the leadership, its differences, the reasons for the split between the "Officials" and the "Provisionals," and the appearance of the Irish National Liberation Army splinter.

Like many other terrorist organizations, the Irish Republican Army, the IRA, has its full share of leadership problems, which are related not only to the campaign in Northern Ireland, but also to those of survival, of individuals pushing for position and power, methods to be used, grassroots support, supplies of arms and money, the "north-south" friction, and others. We hear much about the difficulties of the security forces in both Northern Ireland and the Irish Republic, in their struggle against the IRA, so perhaps for a change we can look at the other side of the fence to examine some of the anxieties, fears, and frustrations of the terrorist leaders themselves. In this article, the expression "IRA" can generally be taken to mean the "Official" IRA, and its two splinters, the "Provisional" IRA, and the Irish National Liberation Army, unless otherwise mentioned.

The IRA, as we have come to know it during the last decade of terrorist activity in Northern Ireland, found its form and constitution in the late 1920s and the 1930s. It differs in some ways from other terrorist organizations with national aims, such as those of the Basques or the Corsicans. Most terrorists have mounted a tiger—they cannot dismount—they know too much, so one significant difference is that IRA members can resign if they wish, or be dismissed as being unsuitable, or for disciplinary reasons. In this respect the IRA is something like a club, a trade union, or even a volunteer conventional army. Members can, of course, be "knee-capped," or even eliminated, if they transgress the IRA code.

The IRA practice has been not to retain a man against his will, since it recognizes that terrorism is a young man's game, and that as he gets older he may want to marry and settle down, start his own business, or get a regular job. He may disagree with official policy, or may have outgrown his youthful idealism, or simply has had enough. The IRA recognizes that a discontented man can become an embittered canker, and that it is best to part on friendly terms. Men who leave the IRA are seldom taken back, but they are left alone, and not penalized, or used in any way, having the sole obligation to keep their mouths shut, and not to become informers. There are many hundreds, even thousands, who if they wished could write after their names "IRA (Rtd)" in the military manner.

## Collective Leadership

The IRA survived the Irish Civil War, of 1923–24, and the subsequent efforts at suppression by the Irish Free State government, as small, underground units, scattered countrywide, meeting and training secretly. Each IRA unit, no matter how small, and some were down to less than half a dozen members, was entitled to send a delegate to the IRA Conventions, usually held annually, or sometimes more frequently, and all had an equal single vote. At the Conventions twelve members were elected to form the Executive Committee, and as in other political organizations, there was at times intriguing and lobbying aplenty. Sean MacStiofean has alleged[1] that at the IRA Convention held in December 1969, at which his proposals were defeated, and which caused him to form the breakaway "Provisional" IRA, many delegates were

[1] Sean MacStiofean, *Memoirs of a Revolutionary*, Gordon & Cremonesi, London, 1975.

either not informed of the time and location of the Convention in time, or were deliberately kept away.

The elected Executive Committee retired to choose seven of its members to form the "Army Council," which was the collective leadership. One member of the Council became the Chief of Staff, and two others the Adjutant-General and the Quartermaster General; they were the three most powerful men in the movement. The Chief of Staff, as chief executive, had considerable powers, but could be outvoted in Council. Thus it was claimed that the IRA was a democratically run organization. The IRA always thought of itself as an "army," and used military titles, designations, and formations.

Over the years of success and failure, intrigue abounded, as some Chiefs of Staff schemed for absolute power, tried to pack the Army Council with their nominees, while others were eased out or even summarily dismissed, or worse could happen to them. In 1941, many IRA leaders were arrested in Dublin by the Garda, whereupon the Adjutant-General, Sean McCaughey, a Northerner, and some of his Northern colleagues, seized the Chief of Staff, Stephen Hayes, whom they suspected of being the informer, held him in a house, tortured him to extract confessions that proved to be false, and then sentenced him to death by court martial. Hayes managed to escape and told his story to the police. Both Hayes and McCaughey were imprisoned. Hayes was released to the anonymity of civilian life in 1946, while McCaughey died that year in prison, while on a hunger strike. One critic[2] of MacStiofean, who was Chief of Staff of the Provisionals from 1969 until 1972, alleged there was talk of killing him to get rid of him as he had become so callously blood-thirsty. However, MacStiofean was eventually arrested and imprisoned. He went on a 59-day hunger strike, was eventually released, and was eased out of the IRA. He had lost face as a "failed martyr."

Sometimes Chiefs of Staff came and went quickly, usually because they were arrested; for example, during the period between 1941 and 1946, a new one had to be appointed about every six months on the average. On the other hand, some reigned longer. Tony Magan was Chief of Staff for eight years (1946-1954), and Cathal Goulding, Chief of Staff of the Official IRA, who was appointed in 1962, is still going strong.

[2]Maria McGuire, *To Take Arms*, Macmillan, London, 1973.

## Legality

IRA leaders are obsessed with the "legality" of their cause and their
appointments, because they feel, that in a Catholic country, with a
Catholic membership, they need the Church's blessing, or more accurately, they want to avoid its condemnation and excommunication,
which did so much to defeat the IRA in the 1920s. They need confidence
that they are fighting a "just war," and so have "a license to kill." In
early 1938, Sean Russell, a former Director of IRA Intelligence, who
had been expelled for his left-wing views, was reinstated in the IRA by a
newly elected Army Council, and appointed Chief of Staff. He immediately put the notorious "S Plan" into operation, for a bombing
campaign in England. There were doubts about the legality of his
appointment, so he brought together the remaining Sinn Fein members
of the Second Dail, of 1919, which Republicans regarded as the last
legal one, having been swept aside by force of Free State arms. In
December 1938, he persuaded them to sign a document, known as the
"IRA-Dail Treaty," in Dublin, which formally handed over their powers to the IRA in Convention. At the next IRA Convention he
"legalized" his appointment. MacStiofean sought legality for his
"Provisional" organization at the Sinn Fein Convention in January
1970, but failed.

At that Sinn Fein Convention, Tom Maguire, the last surviving
member of the Second Dail, declared that it was wrong to abolish the
policy of "abstentionism," and so the decision of the IRA Convention
was reversed. The Sinn Fein had been putting up candidates at elections
for the Dail, Stormont, and even Westminster for years, but when
winning, they did not take their seats. The Official IRA had tried to
change that.

## The IRA Objective

All sections of the IRA seem to have been steadily united in their
ultimate objective, which is a United Ireland, but differ on the methods
by which this is to be accomplished, and what sort of a United Ireland it
should be. The Official IRA is Marxist in character and aim, and its
"front" organization is now called the "Sinn Fein—The Workers
Party." It wants to follow the classic Communist pattern of preparing

the masses for revolution, and to establish a Socialist regime and way of life in Ireland. Its philosophy is that if the masses are not ready and conditioned for revolution, the revolution must be postponed until they are. This was the case in 1968 and 1969, when the leadership refused to let the IRA as a body take part in, and take advantage of, the civil rights movement that was sweeping across Northern Ireland. Cathal Goulding, the Chief of Staff, said that "the time is not yet ripe for military action."

The Provisional IRA is the militant organization that seeks to achieve a United Ireland by terrorist means. When this is achieved, if it ever is, the leadership wants a Social Democratic government on the West European pattern. The Irish National Liberation Army wants to achieve a Communist-type revolution by violence. All sections of the IRA want to eliminate the Dublin government.

## The Social Conscience

Since the 1930s there have been two distinct pressure groups within the IRA, one that wants military action, and the other that somehow wants to associate itself with the people in a Communist manner. This Socialist complex, or conscience, developed in the 1930s, in the "colored shirt era," of Hitler's Brown Shirts, and of Mussolini's and Mosley's Black Shirts. In Ireland, General O'Duffy organized his Fascist-type Blue Shirts, and the IRA, which was just coming to life again, went into action against them.

When the Spanish Civil War broke out in 1936, Frank Ryan, a member of the IRA Council, who held strong left-wing views, took a number of IRA men with him to Spain, where they fought in the James Connolly Battalion, of the Abraham Lincoln Brigade, of the International Brigade. Ryan was captured by the Spanish Nationalists and imprisoned, but eventually released to Germany, where he was joined by Sean Russell, the IRA Chief of Staff, who in 1939, had gone to the United States on a fund-raising tour, and when World War II began went to Germany to seek support for the IRA.

In August 1940, both Ryan and Russell were being taken by German submarine back to Ireland, when Russell died, and was buried at sea. Ryan was taken back to Germany. It was almost a repeat of the Sir Roger Casement incident of 1916. The conflicting issue of a Socialist-type revolution and military action remained a divisive factor in the IRA, and was the basic cause of the split in 1969, of the movement into the Officials and the Provisionals.

## Struggles and Splits

There were also many power struggles, personality clashes, and quarrels within the leadership of the IRA. It was the policy of the IRA that once a man who held any appointment was arrested, he was replaced within the movement by someone else, and that happened to several Chiefs of Staff. One Chief of Staff who would not accept this ruling was Tony Magan, who was arrested in 1954 and detained with other IRA prisoners in the Curragh Internment Camp. He smuggled notes out to Sean Cronin, who had been appointed in his place, telling him how to run the Northern Campaign that was just starting. Cronin ignored them. On his later release, Magan attempted to have Cronin tried by court martial for disobeying orders. Eventually Magan was dismissed from the IRA.

Personality clashes have caused the IRA to splinter in the past; for example, in October 1951, when Liam Kelly, a Northerner, was dismissed from the IRA by Chief of Staff Magan, with his followers, Kelly formed his own Saor Uladh (Free Ulster) group, which took part in the Northern Campaign, and cooperated with the IRA. Another was Joe Christle, and extrovert student, who was dismissed from the IRA by the Chief of Staff in 1956, for being too flamboyant, so he formed a breakaway movement, taking with him most of the Dublin units, and the GHQ staff.

## North-South Friction

Dating from the World War II period, an increasing number of "Northerners" gained senior positions in the IRA, and there was always a certain amount of suspicion and friction between them and the seemingly more easy-going "Southerners." As Northern Ireland, in the IRA view at least, was still "occupied by the enemy," somewhat naturally it was the focus of IRA dynamism. The Northerners felt that not enough priority and attention were given to the IRA in Northern Ireland. The Northerners generally had a brisker attitude and wanted action, which was why so many deserted the Officials and joined the Provisionals.

One other point caused Northern irritation, and that was the Gaelic language, taught in schools in the south, which many Republicans set great store by. MacStiofean, an Englishman who had learned Gaelic in prison, and had Gaelicized his name, used it on every possible occasion, especially in his home. When Northern leaders came to meet him there, they complained they could not understand a word that was spoken, and suspected him of speaking in Gaelic deliberately to confuse them. Gaelic is not taught in Northern schools, not even Catholic ones.

## Northern Leadership

Once the Provisional IRA became a separate and viable organization and moved into action in 1970, it was inevitable that Northern leaders were elected to the Provisional Executive Committee and the Army Council, where they made their presence felt. David O'Connell was Chief of Staff for a couple of years after MacStiofean was arrested, and he pursued similar violent tactics, which had been culled from studies of recent insurgent campaigns in Cyprus, Aden, and Algeria and were based mainly on the bomb and the bullet. In short, he carried out a form of guerrilla warfare.

In 1975, Gerry Adams, a Northerner, became Provisional IRA Chief of Staff, and O'Connell concentrated on political work with the Provisional Sinn Fein. He grouped around him a number of other Northernners, all of whom had distinguished themselves in the fighting in Northern Ireland. They included Joe Cahill, Ivor Bell, Martin McGuiness, Seamus Twomey, Brian Keenan, and others who packed the Army Council. Apart from short individual spells of absence in detention, this same tight group still runs the Provisional IRA today. Although Dublin is the seat of the GHQ, and the Provisional Sinn Fein HQ, at Kevin Street, Dublin, is still the mouthpiece, the control of the Provisional IRA is firmly in Northern hands.

## Secret Cells

During 1975 and 1976, the security forces in Northern Ireland were remarkably successful in arresting Provisional leaders at all levels. Clearly, informers were at work, the long-time curse of the IRA. The security forces thought they were beginning to get on top of the terrorist problem, and for a while they were. The Northern junta saw that their

organization and tactics were suspect, so they turned away from guerrilla warfare and studied the international terrorist groups that began to
receive world publicity for their exploits, such as the Baader-Meinhof
Gang, the Red Brigades, and the Palestinian terrorist factions, and
decided to adopt certain of their features.

During 1977, and 1978, the old military-type structure of the Provisional IRA, of brigades, battalions, and companies, was torn down, and
suitable manpower reformed into small, four or six-man (and woman)
secret cells, in which members only knew one another. A vertical chain
of command was formed in which only the cell leader knew his next
higher echelon. In this way it was hoped to eliminate the informer. This
drastic reorganization took two years to accomplish, during which the
security forces were congratulating themselves that they were at last
slowly winning the war against terrorism in Northern Ireland. Both the
Garda in the Irish Republic and the security forces in Northern Ireland
admitted their sources of information had practically dried up. The
shock came in 1979, when acts of terrorism suddenly increased in
volume.

## Doubts and Difficulties

One danger to the present Provisional leadership, which at the moment
seems firm and united, may be dissension over the secret-cell organization, which does not somehow seem to entirely suit the Irish character,
and already there are mutterings against it. Most IRA men like the ''old
army'' structure better, together with the semi-secret guerrilla warfare.
The present secret cells have to host specialist teams, of bombers,
gunmen, and executioners, who suddenly appear, strike, and then
disappear, and whose arrogance and secretiveness make them locally
unpopular. Grass-roots volunteers like to be kept in the picture. The
secret-cell system proved successful in small, highly sophisticated terrorist groups, but the Provisional leadership has to worry whether it is
suitable in the long term in an organization numbering many hundreds of
people. The ''army'' aspect of the IRA always gave members a certain
dignity and prestige, which the secret-cell organization lacks. Another
possibility is that Gerry Adams, or other members of his Army Council,
may be arrested, or may even be pushed out by others who may have
different ideas on how the Provisionals should operate.

As the terrorist campaign continues, dissident factions may form and splinter from the Provisional IRA. Also, there may be fighting between the Irish National Liberation Army and the Provisionals, over recruits, money, arms, and territory. In the early 1970s the Officials and the Provisionals fought each other like gangster mobs, and in 1972 full-scale war between them was only narrowly averted. Survival and unity are leadership problems.

The Provisionals' leadership worries about its precarious arms supply lines, which have frequently been disrupted by discoveries of cargoes of illicit arms at Dublin, in Holland, and elsewhere. Arms still get through, but they are becoming much more difficult to obtain and to tranship to Northern Ireland. The American sources are drying up, and the Middle East ones are unreliable. MacStiofean has alleged that the intelligence agencies of Britain, America, Russia, and several other countries have been working together to prevent illegal arms reaching Ireland.

The Provisionals' leadership is beginning to have financial worries too, as the dollars, for so many years collected from Irish-Americans and sent to Ireland, are drying up. Jack Lynch, the former Prime Minister of the Irish Republic and the present Prime Minister, Mr. Charles Haughey, who are dedicated to uniting Ireland by peaceful means, and also certain prominent American politicians, are openly discouraging Irish-Americans from contributing money to "front organizations," since it will end up in the IRA coffers. The bank and other robberies in the Irish Republic, which have netted the IRA over £4 million during the last three years, cannot be expected to continue, as the Irish government must soon be introducing special countermeasures to stop this IRA source of income. Without arms and money, the IRA could not keep up its present terrorist momentum.

Another main anxiety is the possible loss of the support of the Catholic communities in Northern Ireland, which was obtained, and retained, by intimidation alone. The Catholic communities in Belfast and Derry must be heartily sick of IRA domination and protection rackets, but as yet none dare say so. Any IRA setback, or signs that it might be losing out against the security forces, might start a ground swell of opposition, when information would once again flow in to the police and IRA demands may begin to be resisted. Peace movements have appeared in Northern Ireland, but they have been generally negated by IRA "out-of-television-camera range" activities.

The IRA leadership knows that as long as the border remains open and the Irish Republic can be used as a sanctuary, a base, and a Ho Chi Minh Trail the security forces in Northern Ireland cannot defeat them. The sanctuary may be an uneasy one, as IRA members may be detained, but the ''100 or so'' men wanted by the Royal Ulster Constabulary for terrorist crimes in the North know they will never be extradited. But the former tolerance of the IRA in certain influential circles in the South seems to be evaporating, and today the IRA is in dread of a closer liaison between Northern Ireland and Irish Republic security forces in the border areas.

# Terror in Ireland— and Britain's Response

## Merlyn Rees

*Abstract*    Reacting to the last of four distinct terrorist campaigns in Northern Ireland, the British Parliament in 1973 passed the Northern Ireland (Emergency Provisions) Act, which was amended in 1974. The act marks the first time in United Kingdom statute law that terrorism is defined as the use of violence for political ends. British efforts are aimed at the development of the police to the point where the military is no longer required. Terroristic acts in Great Britain, usually connected with Northern Irish affairs, have led to the introduction of the Prevention of Terrorism (Temporary Provisions) Act, the powers of which are also described in this paper. The author also discusses the problem of the safeguarding of civil liberties as well as the European Convention on the Suppression of Terrorism, drawn up by the Council of Europe.

## Emergency Provisions in Northern Ireland

The use of violence for political ends has been a feature of Irish history for over two hundred years. Since the establishment of Northern Ireland itself in 1920 there have been four distinct terrorist campaigns; in the 1920s, during the 1939–45 world war, between 1956 and 1962, and the present campaign which began in 1969. In 1972, following the prorogation of the Northern Ireland Parliament and the imposition of direct rule from Westminster, the United Kingdom Government appointed a

Committee under the chairmanship of Lord Diplock, the eminent jurist, to consider "what arrangements for the administration of justice in Northern Ireland could be made in order to deal more efficiently with terrorist organizations. . . ." Diplock found that the main obstacle to dealing with terrorists in the ordinary courts was the intimidation of jurors and witnesses by terrorist organizations, and the principal recommendations in his report were embodied in the Northern Ireland (Emergency Provisions) Act 1973. This provided for:

- all terrorist-type offences to be categorized as "scheduled" offences;
- trials of scheduled offences to be by a senior judge, sitting alone, but with more than the usual rights of appeal;
- bail in scheduled cases to be given only by the High Court (rather than by a magistrate) and then only if stringent precautions were made;
- the arrest without warrant and detention by the police for up to 72 hours of any person suspected of being a terrorist (the normal requirement in Northern Ireland is that arrested persons must be brought before a court within 48 hours of arrest);
- the arrest and detention of a suspect for up to 4 hours by members of the Army;
- wide powers of search and seizure by members of the security forces;
- reversal of the normal onus of proof in relation to offences of possession of arms and explosives;
- a fresh system of detention by the executive. (Detention orders could be made by the Secretary of State on the basis of information which the security forces believed to be valid, whereas conviction for offences under the normal criminal law is of course on the basis of evidence tested in court. I should add that, although the emergency legislation in Northern Ireland still provides for a system of detention, this power has not been used since 1975; all persons in custody in Northern Ireland have thus been convicted of criminal offences or are awaiting trial for criminal offences.)

For the first time in United Kingdom statute law, terrorism was defined as the use of violence for political ends, including any use of violence for the purpose of putting the public in fear. This 1973 Act was itself subject to review in 1974 by a Committee headed by Lord Gardiner, another eminent jurist, whose task was to consider the anti-terrorist measures in the context of civil liberties and human rights. The main changes which were made as a result of their report were in regard to the procedures for detention which, as I have said, is no longer in use.

Any legislation of this kind clearly necessitates some loss of liberty and human freedom. The powers which have evolved nevertheless represent a determination by successive British Governments that such legislation will depart as little as possible from internationally agreed principles and from the traditions of British justice. The aim is to ensure both that the security forces have every assistance in their task of bringing terrorists before the courts and that the integrity of the legal system is maintained.

Moving on from the legislation itself, security policy in Northern Ireland has been and continues to be based on the fair and effective enforcement of the law. At the heart of the policy is a determination to develop the effectiveness and acceptance of the police to the point where a military involvement in the maintenance of law and order is no longer required. Much progress has been made; the strength of the Royal Ulster Constabulary now stands at more than 6,000 compared with 3,800 in 1970, and there have also been significant organizational changes in the force. Fundamental to this security policy is the belief that terrorists are criminals under the law, they are prosecuted for criminal offences and not for the political beliefs that they may hold.

## Terrorism in Great Britain

I now turn to the position in the rest of the United Kingdom. Here, although the incidence of terrorism has not been as extensive as in Northern Ireland, it has been bad enough. In the past 7 years there have been approximately 300 terrorist incidents in Great Britain (that is England, Wales and Scotland) which have resulted in the deaths of 75 people and over ten times as many injured. The overwhelming majority of these incidents have been connected with the situation in Northern Ireland. It was after a particularly horrific example—an attack on two public houses in Birmingham in 1974 which killed 21 people—that the Government introduced the Prevention of Terrorism (Temporary Provisions) Act.

The Act (and its subordinant legislation) is intended to prevent acts of terrorism connected with Northern Irish affairs. To this end it provides two important powers. The first is the power given to the Home Secretary to exclude a person from Great Britain or from the United Kingdom as a whole. (The Secretary of State for Northern Ireland is also given similar power to exclude a person from Northern Ireland or the United Kingdom.) The Home Secretary or his Northern Ireland counterpart may exercise this power only if he is satisfied that the person is, or has been, concerned in the commission, preparation or instigation of acts of terrorism, or is attempting, or may attempt, to enter the country for that purpose. This is an executive power which does not involve court procedures, and could not because the information on which the Home Secretary takes his decision is usually intelligence information which could not be revealed in open court. There is provision in the legislation for a person to make representations against exclusion which are considered by independent advisers appointed under the Act. But the final responsibility for deciding whether to exclude rests with the Home Secretary.

The second important power provided is the power to detain a person for up to a maximum of seven days without bringing him before a court. The police are empowered to arrest a person without a warrant if they reasonably suspect that he has committed an offence under the Act or is involved in acts of terrorism; and they may detain such a person on their own authority for up to 48 hours. The Home Secretary may extend the period of detention to a maximum of seven days in all. The purpose of this power of detention is to give the police time to make enquiries about the person detained in order to decide whether to apply to the Home Secretary for an exclusion order or to charge the person and bring him before the courts.

These are the most important parts of the legislation. It also provides for the proscription in Great Britain of organizations which the Home Secretary considers are concerned in terrorism in the United Kingdom connected with Northern Irish affairs. (A similar power to proscribe organizations in Northern Ireland is contained in other legislation.) At present, only the IRA is proscribed in Great Britain because it is that organization which has been responsible for most of the acts of terrorism which have taken place in Great Britain. In Northern Ireland 7 organizations are proscribed. It is an offence to further the aims of a proscribed organization. It is also an offence under the Prevention of Terrorism Act to raise money for acts of terrorism connected with Northern Ireland but unrelated to proscribed organizations, and to fail to disclose to the police information about terrorism connected with Northern Irish affairs. Finally, I should mention that regulations made under the Act lay down a framework of controls at ports. These controls give the police power to examine, search and detain people at ports for the purpose of determining whether they are involved in terrorism or have committed an offence under the Act.

## How to Preserve Civil Liberties?

It will be apparent from what I have said that in responding to the threat from terrorism we have been compelled to make some inroads into our civil liberties.

This brings me to the most important question which this conference is concerned with, namely, the conflict between the preservation of civil liberties and the protection of lives and property from terrorist attack. I use the word "conflict" deliberately. There is no way in which we can take powers to deal with terrorism without at the same time diminishing the ordinary, innocent citizen's own freedom. The terrorist knows this and rejoices at every such measure introduced. For in a democratic society the terrorist's aim (whatever his political coloration) is to discredit the Government. He tries to do this first by sowing seeds of doubt about the Government's capacity to defend its citizens and then, more insidiously, by trying to bring about the steady erosion of civil liberties to a point where the Government and society's commitment to democratic values is fatally weakened.

This means that those of us who are caught in this "conflict" have to keep a steady nerve. We must be especially alive to the addictive effect of anti-terrorist measures—once introduced into the body politic it is difficult to contemplate giving them up. It is specifically in order to prevent what I might call entrenchment by stealth that the Northern Ireland Emergency Provisions legislation has to be approved by both Houses of Parliament every 6 months. The Prevention of Terrorism Act has similarly to be approved, every 12 months, if it is to continue in force. By this means we hope that we can keep alive the realization that these measures are emergency ones only and should be temporary.

The problems of Northern Ireland are unique and I have no doubt that there have to be political as well as security solutions to them. Many other countries in the West are increasingly finding that their democratic institutions are under attack by terrorist groups of one complexion or another. The motivation of terrorists may differ from country to country, but their ultimate aim is the same: to overthrow by violence the democratically elected government and to impose their own views upon the public.

## European Convention on Suppression of Terrorism

Such methods must not be allowed to prevail, and if they are not to do so it is clearly necessary for democratic governments to cooperate in measures to ensure that those who commit terrorist acts are brought to justice. An example of such cooperation is the European Convention on the Suppression of Terrorism, drawn up by the Council of Europe, and concluded in 1977. The United Kingdom has ratified that Convention without reservation by means of the Suppression of Terrorism Act 1978. Briefly, the Convention provides that certain terrorist-type offences are not to be regarded as political offences for the purpose of extradition between contracting states. The Convention also embodies the requirement to consider prosecution in cases where extradition is refused. It is designed to ensure so far as possible that terrorists cannot escape justice by taking refuge outside the country where they committed their offences and pleading that those offences were politically motivated as a defense against extradition. I should say that neither the Convention nor our own Act is a threat to genuine political refugees, whose interests are properly safeguarded. A recent development has been the drawing up of an agreement among the member states of the EEC concerning the operation of the Convention among themselves until such time as all of them should have ratified it without reservation. As well as their practical value, agreements of this kind demonstrate the determination of democratic governments not to capitulate to terrorism.

# Another Final Battle on the Stage of History

## Jillian Becker

Author, London

*Abstract*     Taking its point of departure in remarks made by Ulrike Meinhof during the 1972 trial in West Germany of Horst Mahler, this paper goes on to examine some of the ideas and assumptions of the members of the terrorist group to which he belonged. Meinhof's as well as Mahler's views of the Jews in Germany and their fate, including their charge of a conspiracy on the part of the malevolent powers, are quoted and make it clear that as terrorists they conformed to a grandiose millenarian tradition. This millenarian tradition has had a long history in Germany, comprising anarchic, egalitarian, and communistic elements. Examples are the followers of John Hus and Thomas Müntzer. The need for group identification is also strong in the millenarians of the present day who believe in and act unquestioningly upon tenets such as those of terrorist groups like the Red Army Faction which, fortunately, has not gained the following of such predecessors as Hitler's Third Reich.

In December 1972, Horst Mahler, a lawyer who had organized a terrorist group in West Germany in 1969 and was arrested in October 1970, was brought to trial in Berlin. He was charged with conspiracy to commit crimes and with armed robbery. One of the witnesses called at the trial was Mahler's erstwhile accomplice, Ulrike Meinhof, who had been arrested some five months earlier, in June 1972, and was awaiting trial on charges of armed robbery, conspiracy, murder, and attempted murder.

She appeared in court on the 27th day of Mahler's trial.[1] She refused to sit in the place reserved for witnesses. The Presiding Judge warned her that if she would not cooperate, she would be seated in a special plate-glass box which had been installed for another witness, Karl-Heinz Ruhland, who needed protection because he had agreed to give evidence against the group to which he had himself once belonged.

Meinhof replied: "You threaten me with your Eichmann box, you fascist, you pig. You want to lock anti-fascists into that box in which Genscher [Federal Minister of the Interior] belongs."

The court informed her of her rights and duties as a witness. Her only response was, "Blah! Blah!"

She was threatened with a fine.

"All right," she said. "Just get on with it."

Asked her profession she replied, "Anti-fascist."

She was reminded that she must tell the truth.

Meinhof: "We always tell the truth. We are here because we can no longer endure your lying."

In giving her evidence, she said, "I am related to Horst Mahler. We were both born in the 30s; we had the same family background; we both grew up during the Second World War."

The Judge asked whether they were blood relations.

Meinhof: "Oh, of course, blood, that is what you want."

The trial proceeded, and suddenly Meinhof screamed out, "There you are waffling about bank robbery, while experiments on human beings are being conducted in Cologne-Ossendorf!" Hysterically she complained about the "inhuman conditions of detention" to which Astrid Proll, she said, was being subjected at Ossendorf, "a penal institution, whose symbol is a smokestack." She said, "You pigs obviously want a prominent suicide."

The Presiding Judge: "Frau Meinhof is obviously very agitated."

Meinhof: "I have been agitated for thirty-eight years now, over the state of affairs in Germany."

Mahler was given permission to question Meinhof. He told her that he "had to play this shit game" but he was concerned with "making it difficult for them to suppress certain things." And he began to read aloud from an underground publication. The court had rejected his application to read it out loud, so now he wanted to use it to question her.

Amicably, the Presiding Judge suggested that he could hand it to the journalists if he wanted it made public, upon which Mahler suggested that the Judge himself read it aloud. The Judge declined, and Mahler proceeded to read the document.

The polemical declaration which Mahler read was being circulated in 1973 as an "RAF" (Red Army Faction) underground publication under the title *The Action of the Black September in Munich—on the strategy of the anti-imperialist struggle*. It was almost certainly written by Mahler himself. It argued a point of view of which the following is a representative extract:

> With their action in the Olympic village, they [the Arab terrorists who killed the Israeli athletes] have carried the apparently only local conflict between the imperialist metropolis Israel and the Palestinians from the periphery of the system to the center—they have forced the character-masks of the Federal Republic law-and-order-state to take off the makeup and appear as what all character-masks of imperialism objectively are: warring parties against the freedom movements of the Thirld World—in the final analysis: extermination strategists and fascists.

The action, Mahler asserted, was "anti-fascist . . . because it was in memory of the 1936 Olympics." And he proceeded: "Israel weeps crocodile tears. It has burned up its sportsmen like the Nazis did the Jews—incendiary material for the imperialist extermination policy."

Ulrike Meinhof did not entirely agree with all that Mahler said. She interrupted his reading several times with comments such as, "That is not a perfect theory, though it does go something along those lines." And eventually she put what she believed was the right theory, concerning the Jews—at present, and in Nazi Germany—in her own words: "Without pronouncing the German people 'not guilty' of fascism—for the people truly did not know what went on in the concentration camps—we cannot mobilize them for our revolutionary struggle."

After the war, she said, the Left had reacted to fascism in a "careless, stupid, and brazen manner." Personalities were pushed into the foreground, but no deeper view was taken. "How was Auschwitz possible, what was anti-Semitism?" That should have been cleared up then [by "the Left"] instead of its concurring in the view that Auschwitz was the expression of evil.

"That's the worst of it," she said, "that we all agreed on that, Communists along with the others."

But now, she asserted, she herself had recognized that anti-Semitism in its essence is anti-capitalism. It used the hatred of the people of their dependence on money as a medium of exchange, their longing for communism.

"Auschwitz," she said, "means that six million Jews were murdered and carted on to the rubbish dumps of Europe for being that which was maintained of them—Money-Jews."

What had happened, she said, was that "finance capital" and banks, "the hard core of the system of imperialism and capitalism," had diverted the people's hatred of money and exploitation away from themselves and on to the Jews. Not to have made these connections clear was the failure of the Left, of the Communists. The Germans were anti-Semitic, and therefore they were supporters of the RAF. Only they did not know it, because they had not been pronounced "not guilty" of fascism, of murdering Jews, and had not been told that anti-Semitism was actually hatred of capitalism.

Because they had not been told that hatred of the Jews was actually hatred of capitalism, the German people had failed to support the Red Army Faction. But now she was making it clear, and it was on these grounds that the action of the Black September in Munich was to be praised.

However, she went on to claim a "historical identity" with the Jews of the Warsaw ghetto, who had "tried without arms to start a rebellion and then let themselves be butchered." "And with that," she said, "we have broken through the whole 'blah-blah.' "

Mahler wanted to continue reading from his document, but Meinhof said she had had enough. "I'm fed up now. I want to go now." And she pretended to faint. She was asked whether she wanted something to drink but she said no, she only wanted to leave, and with the permission of the court she embraced Mahler and was led out.

Ulrike Meinhof was clearly in no state to put forward a reasoned argument at the Mahler trial, and she made no great effort to do so. She declaimed histrionically rather than explained her views: she was "acting to the gallery." But at the best of times she was not a clear thinker; and her confusion in court was symptomatic, not merely of temporary emotional disturbance, but of character; and what she revealed were certain characteristic assumptions which are, for that very reason, particularly interesting.

The ideology which Meinhof and her associates had embraced, "world communist revolution," condemned Israel as an arm of American "imperialism," and Zionism as racism.[2] But the making of a case against the Israelis presented them with peculiar difficulties; for they were the self-appointed champions and leaders of the German "people" in an armed revolution which they hoped to have launched with their acts of terrorism.[3] And in order to justify morally the violent crimes with which they were charged, Meinhof and her fellow terrorists represented themselves as righteous fighters against the same sort of regime as had prevailed in Germany during the Third Reich; and insisted they were being subjected to the same treatment at the hands of the authorities of the Federal Republic as the Jews at the hands of the Nazis ("experiments are being conducted on human beings"; "a penal institution whose symbol is a smokestack"; Genscher "belongs" in the "Eichmann box").[4]

Not to condemn the treatment of the Jews by their German persecutors would be to deprive themselves of their most cherished propaganda weapon. And the simple expedient, popular with the extreme Left, of making a distinction between the Israelis and the Jews would not quite adequately serve. For unless the German "people" were "pronounced 'not guilty' " of racial persecution of the Jews, they might find the words condemning anyone for "racism" sticking in their throats.

Fortunately for the Red Army Faction, the very ideology which created the difficulty provided them with a solution if only they could apply it. What was necessary for them to do was to reinterpret the history of the Third Reich in such a way as to exonerate the working class of Germany from culpability by putting the blame for the racial persecution and genocide on to other—that is to say the "capitalist" or "exploiting"—classes.

To achieve this, Meinhof's first and obvious recourse was to say that "the people did not know." This she says; but does not after all believe it herself. She goes on to try another explanation: "The people" had indeed hated the Jews. But not *as* Jews. It was rather because "finance capital" had diverted their hatred, which was really a "hatred of their dependence on money as a medium of exchange," away from itself on to the Jews. So when the masses participated in, or connived at, or did not prevent the killing of the six million (assuming now that they did know about it), it was because they had been persuaded that the Jews were representative of economic exploitation and therefore received their just deserts in the extermination camps.

But did Meinhof herself believe that the identification of the Jews with what she regards as economic exploitation was without moral justification or factual foundation? Did she believe that "the people" had been entirely misled, and that they therefore in turn had made a mistake, albeit an honest one? It seems not. What she says is this:

"Auschwitz heisst, das sechs Millionen Juden ermordet und auf die Müllkippen Europas gekarrt wurden als das, als was man sie ausgab— als Geldjuden." (Literal translation: "Auschwitz means that six million Jews were murdered and carted on to the rubbish dumps of Europe as that which was maintained of them—as Money Jews.")

If it is not absolutely clear from this that she herself believed they *were* "Money-Jews," what is by now perfectly clear is that their murder *as "Money-Jews"* is not to her wrong, as it just might have been if they had been murdered *as Jews*. So, if the people did know, and were responsible at all for mass murder, it was not murder purely for reasons of race hatred, which would have been wrong according to the ideology of the Left in the 1970s, but more for reasons of class hatred, which is not wrong: and therefore the people can be "pronounced 'not guilty' " of genocide.[5]

But Meinhof did use the word *"Geldjuden,"* intending it to convey the loathing and contempt it had long carried, and as a sign of race hatred, anti-Semitism, but with an excuse tacked on which reflected both a traditional and a contemporary Communist rationale.

If we can conclude that to Meinhof they *were* "Money-Jews," *were* "finance capital," in the logic which Meinhof did not see or attempt to see, they "diverted" the people's hatred *away from themselves* as "capitalist exploiters" *on to themselves* as Jews! Even Meinhof seems to have been aware that something was wrong with all this. Uneasily she felt—so it appears—that there was still something she ought to say about Jews, about the victims with whom she was, after all, claiming equality of victimization. There was still the very important requirement not to appear as a racist herself. Some Jews must be exempted from condemnation. So with the Jews of the Warsaw ghetto, she claims "fellow feeling."

But it seems that she still felt dissatisfaction with her own argument. And it was probably out of a sense of frustration that obdurate facts continued to give her the lie, and that her own repeated claims to extraordinary humanitarianism were now betrayed and made her want to do violence to all opposing arguments, with words, since she now lacked other weapons: ". . . broken through the whole blah-blah!'' she says.

The idea of conspiracy on the part of malevolent powers who use economic means to oppress the people was implied by Ulrike Meinhof in her speech to the court at Horst Mahler's trial, and she also trotted out that old canard of anti-Semitism that the Jews are such economic oppressors. More explicitly, Mahler himself expressed belief in conspiracy in the declaration he made in his own defense.

He declared:

> You charge me with conspiracy. . . . But you yourself, the gang of General Motors, Ford, Armco, General Electric, ITT, Siemens, AEG, Flick, Quandt, BASF, Springer, Unilever, United Fruit, and certain others—the transnational consortia of capital, all together the imperialistic Monopoly Capital—are the most monstrous criminal association in history. To destroy this with all necessary and obtainable means is a necessity of life for more than 3 billion people.[6] . . . The imperialist system, which presents hell on earth to ever-increasing portions of humanity, may only be defeated by the action of the armed people and not by incantations, moral appeals, and parliamentary trifling. The Red Army Faction has taken up the idea of arming the people. . . .

So he himself desires an international movement for world revolution:[7]

> The imperialist system forms a worldwide unit which transcends national boundaries. . . . Exploitation and repression are globally organized. . . . It is essential to recognize the global configuration of imperialism as the determining condition of the proletarian revolution; only in that way will it become a world revolution.

And Mahler makes it perfectly plain that he and his group are driven by grandiose millenarian ambitions:

> Not with cheap words, but with deeds, have we come to stand on the side of the overwhelming majority of the people, who today all over the world are taking up arms to free themselves from imperialist suppression and any kind of exploitation. . . . This . . . is a world war—it will be the last and at the same time the longest and bloodiest war of history, because the exploiters do

not hesitate to use the most horrendous torture actions to retain their domi-
nance. It is not a war among nations but a war of classes, which will sweep all
national, social, cultural, and religious boundaries and barriers forever from
the stage of history.

The New Left movement whose massive demonstrations of protest
came to a rather abrupt end about 1969 in Europe, a year or so later in
America, and catapulted a few excited and violent people, reluctant to
give up the movement's revolutionary aims, into terrorism, was itself a
millenarian movement.[8] In his important and admirable book, *The
Pursuit of the Millennium,* Norman Cohn writes:

> It is characteristic of this kind of movement that its aims and premises are
> boundless. A social struggle is seen not as a struggle for specific, limited
> objectives, but as an event of unique importance, different in kind from all
> other struggles known to history, a cataclysm from which the world is to
> emerge totally transformed and redeemed. This is the essence of the re-
> current phenomenon or . . . persistent tradition—that we have called "rev-
> olutionary millenarianism.'"[9]

The New Left was of this kind, and so were—or are—its offshoots:
the Red Army Faction, the Movement Second June (Germany); the Red
Brigades, the Armed Proletarian Cells (Italy); the Angry Brigade[10]
(England); the Japanese Red Army; the Weathermen (U.S.A.); and
numerous similar groups in South America.[11]

It seems to me that there are three ways in which traditional millenarian ideas could have reemerged into public life in the 1960s and 1970s so
little changed from their earlier manifestations. First, by direct learning.
Second, as a result of the tradition having soaked, as it were, the culture
of Europe, influencing connotations even of individual words, the
vocabulary of values. Third, by the same sort of fanatical personalities,
driven by the same sort of inner needs, conceiving the same vague
visions and pursuing them in the same way, not imitating, but innately
resembling their millenarian antecedents.

Certainly some of the founders and leaders of the Red Army
Faction—Ulrike Meinhof, Horst Mahler, Gudrun Ensslin, Andreas
Baader—all resembled, in various ways and to differing degrees, mil-
lenarian fanatics of the past.[12]

As for the tradition, it permeated the cultural air which these gently reared, carefully taught, affluent young persons breathed. In Europe as a whole, and Germany in particular, there had been a long history of religious dissent for centuries before the Reformation, often erupting in militant revolt, with leaders proclaiming their battle to be the last on the stage of history, ushering in the Kingdom of Christ, which would last for a thousand years, after which the world would end. They were, they claimed, fighting a righteous battle, fulfilling apocalyptic prophecies (such as the Book of Revelations), and their enemy was Antichrist. Supremely self-righteous, they dreamed of a better world after their victory, usually anarchic, egalitarian, communistic. Many held an ideal of a "return" to a golden age, a simple life, a natural state, Eden: a nostalgia for a condition of innocence, as before the Fall. Antichrist, the enemy, had many legions. Of these the Jews were a part. Avaritia, Luxuria, Dives were working the misery and destruction of suffering humanity, taking the form of clergy, rich townsfolk, some (but not all) lay rulers, and the Jews. In pursuit of peace, love, holy poverty, mercy, happiness, innocence, plenty effortlessly provided, equality and justice, they took up arms, tortured, burned, destroyed, massacred, and used the most extreme forms of terrorism. Oppression, want, tyranny, despair were their actual accomplishments.

The example I choose is that of the Hussites, both because it is typical, and because it seems highly likely that if any of the founders and leaders of the Red Army Faction knew anything directly of an idealistic millenarian movement of the past, Ulrike Meinhof knew of the Hussites; for her foster-mother, Professor Renate Riemeck, wrote an authoritative work on John Hus, the Bohemian religious reformer.

John Hus was burned as a heretic in 1414. But he himself was not an extremist. He taught that the Church should be disobeyed if its decrees contradicted or distorted the law of Christ as revealed in the Scriptures. It was only after his death, and because of it, that he became the figurehead of a rebellious movement. Multitudes of the discontented found a uniting cause in his martyrdom. The most extreme of the Hussites were the Taborites, apocalyptic phantasists, who idealized apostolic poverty and moral purity and believed that they were fighting the hosts of Antichrist and had a divine mission to purify the earth by destroying sinners. Anyone, they held, who was not with them was against them, and must be ruthlessly destroyed. When they had thus cleansed the earth, the millennium would come, and the surviving saints would live together in a community of love, peace, and equality, free from all law, all compulsion, all rents, taxes and dues, with all goods held in common. Thus they had the outline of a new social order, but no program, no defined method of bringing it into being. As anarcho-communist rebels, in pursuit of their classless society, they waged their war against the wealthy town dwellers. And they had ambitions to carry their crusade beyond Bohemia once their communist paradise had been created there, by going out and conquering the rest of the world. "Unfortunately for their social experiment, the Taborite revolutionaries were so preoccupied with common ownership that they altogether ignored the need to produce."[13] Where they did conquer, these thirsters after justice exercised tyrannical power over the common people, harassed and oppressed them and ruthlessly extorted rents, dues, and taxes.

Except that the communist and anarcho-communist groups of recent years, such as the Red Army Faction, failed to gain the great following that earlier movements did, the resemblances are so numerous and clear that it is hardly necessary to list them. The one similarity which might have been disputed by those who are aware of, but have not looked closely into, the proclaimed ideals of the RAF, is that of anti-Semitism. Their claims to being anti-materialistic—thoroughly contradicted by their manifest cupidity[14]—is well known; but their identification of economic oppression, or what they called *Konsumterror,* with "the Jews" was not revealed except, half-involuntarily, by Ulrike Meinhof at Mahler's trial, as I have shown. For the rest: communism or anarcho-communism, anti-capitalism, egalitarianism; vague beliefs in a revolution which will transform everything forever; pacifism, ideals of moral purity; the sort of people they hoped to gather to their cause; lack of a program; world revolution ambitions, the final and most important battle, to be led by them; their own carefully planned martyrdoms; cruel revenge vented on "deviants," as well as merciless cruelty to their declared enemies; their use of terror—all are traditional. Furthermore, such movements usually began in the higher social strata, among the better educated and well-off, so in this too there was a close resemblance between the middle and upper-class terrorists of Europe, America, and Japan in recent years, and earlier millenarians.

The nature of the religious beliefs was not quite the same, though some of our latter-day terrorists had a religious upbringing, and were themselves religious in the common meaning of the word. Gudrun Ensslin, co-leader and founder of the RAF had a rigidly puritan Protestant upbringing, with a pastor father and a Pietist mother. Daily searching of the conscience was prescribed, a perpetual striving for moral perfection, with its necessarily accompanying despair of ever achieving it, and its frequently accompanying intolerance of those who seem happy without even trying to be good. And Ulrike Meinhof not only had parents who were believing Protestants, but had herself, as a student, sought the spiritual refuge of a devout sect. But both Meinhof and Ensslin were religious personalities in a wider meaning of the word. For both, the moral fervor they brought to bear on what they preferred to call political issues was of the religious crusading kind. They and their fellow terrorists in their own and similar movements held the same kind of belief in absolute standards of good, a self-righteous certainty that they were on the side of good, and that they were fighting a vast conspiracy of evil; a simplistic dualism which again puts them in line with many a millenarian crusader of the past.

Millenarian movements were "in no way typical of the efforts which the poor made to improve their lot. *Prophetae* would construct their apocalyptic lore. . . . That lore would be purveyed to the poor—and the result would be something that was at once a revolutionary movement and an outburst of quasi-religious salvationism."[15] Indeed, it could happen that such a *propheta* would step into a genuinely political conflict and turn it into a millenarian disaster. The German Peasants' Revolt was in the first instance a political and not a millenarian revolt.[16] When Thomas Müntzer and Niklas Storch stepped in to encourage the peasants to overthrow the princes of Saxony—incidentally two exceptionally tolerant princes,[17] the Elector Frederick and Duke John—with a doctrine of social revolution, complaining that the princes were "too rich," they gained them nothing, but only nudged them to their own destruction. When Philip of Hesse went, contemptuously, to do battle with them, Müntzer told the peasants that God was on their side, a miracle would happen, he would "catch the cannonballs in the sleeves of his cloak."[18] But the cannonballs found their mark, the revolt collapsed, and Müntzer fled and hid, but was found, tortured, and beheaded.

From Engels down to the Communist historians of today—Russian as well as

German—Marxists have inflated Müntzer into a giant symbol, a prodigious hero in the history of the "class war." This is a naive view, and one which non-Marxist historians have countered easily enough by pointing to the essentially mystical nature of Müntzer's preoccupations, his general indifference to the material welfare of the poor. Yet it may be suggested that this point too can be over-emphasized. Müntzer was a *propheta* obsessed by eschatological phantasies which he attempted to translate into reality by exploiting social discontent. Perhaps after all it is a sound instinct that has led Marxists to claim him for their own.[19]

Müntzer was venerated by the Anabaptists, whose movement spread in the years following the Peasants' Revolt. It too was an egalitarian and communist millenarian movement. Its "King" and "Messiah of the Last Days," John Leyden, ruled tyrannically over his terrorized flock in the town of Münster. A handsome, swaggering man, who liked to arrange real life as if it were being presented in a theater, and who had been unable to hold an ordinary job, he had more than a little in common with Andreas Baader. When he and his two closest henchmen were at last defeated by the armies of the Bishop of Münster besieging the town, they were tortured to death, and put in cages hung from the church steeple. They hang there to this day, and were hanging there when Ulrike Meinhof went to Münster to study at the University, and edited a short-lived periodical in support of the Peace Movement in the late 1950s.

If the Communists have Müntzer as one of their favorite German chiliast *prophetae,* the Nazis had theirs too. An unknown revolutionary of the early sixteenth century wrote *The Book of a Hundred Chapters.* In it we find that "the route to the Millennium leads through massacre and terror."[20] He wanted to lead a crusade against the rich, after which equality and communal ownership would come into being as the new justice. He combined this belief with fervent nationalism. "The Germans once held the whole world in their hands and will do so again, and with more power than ever."

Cohn writes:

In these phantasies the crude nationalism of a half-educated intellectual erupted into the tradition of popular eschatology. The result is almost uncannily similar to the phantasies which were the core of National Socialist "ideology". . . . There is the same belief in a primitive German culture in which the divine will was once realized and which throughout history had been the source of all good—which was later undermined by a conspiracy of capitalists, inferior, non-German people and the Church of Rome—which must now be restored by a new aristocracy, of humble birth but truly German in soul, under a God-sent saviour who is at once a political leader and a new Christ. It is all there—and so were the offensives in West and East—the terror wielded both as an instrument of policy for its own sake—the biggest massacres in history—in fact everything except the final consummation of the world-empire, which, in Hitler's words, was to last a thousand years.[21]

It may seem that nationalism was one element of the German millenarian tradition that had disappeared by the time the RAF came along, if by "nationalism" one means exaggerated patriotism. German nationalist fervor had, understandably, abated after the Second World War. But the need for group identification was nevertheless strong in these latter-day millenarians. They were people who needed to be part of a gang, who shirked individual responsibility. (Notice Meinhof's need to claim relationship with Mahler. And Gudrun Ensslin told her sister that her "real" siblings were Petra Schelm and Thomas Weissbecker, two of her dead comrades.) They all believed ardently that the collective was of much greater importance than the individual:[22] devotees of international rather than national socialism.

One final example of millenarianism in the past is worth mentioning, for it had a bearing in our century on both Nazi and Marxist ideology.

In the thirteenth century, Joachim of Fiore "elaborated an interpretation of history as an ascent through three successive ages"[23]—the Third Age, a kind of heaven on earth, enduring until the Last Judgment. He added ideas of communism, apocalypse, and the return of a golden age.

"The long-term, indirect influence of Joachim's speculations can be traced right down to the present day, and most clearly in certain 'philosophies of history,' " writes Cohn. He instances the theories of historical evolution of Hegel and others among the German Idealists, and the Marxian dialectic of the three stages of primitive communism, class society, and communism regained. "And," he writes, "it is no less true . . . that the phrase 'the Third Reich'. . . would have had but little emotional significance if the phantasy of the third and most glorious dispensation had not, over the centuries, entered into the common stock of European social mythologies."[24]

The Third Reich was to last a thousand years in the prophecy of Hitler. It lasted only a dozen, but its millenarian leader did gain a large following. Fortunately, the crusades of the RAF and its resemblers of recent years gained no following at all, and can have very little significance even in the history of such movements.

# Notes

1. This account of the proceedings is taken largely from the *Frankfurter Allgemeine Zeitung* of December 15, 1972. Other newspaper accounts are briefer, but serve to confirm the facts sufficiently.

2. In *The Economic War Against the Jews,* (Corgi, London, 1979), Terence Prittie and Walter Henry Nelson write: ''Anti-Zionism has been a convenience for bigots, for it permits the anti-semites to pose as anti-Israeli, while denying any anti-Jewish bias.'' (p. 172.) They substantiate this very fully, and also supply ample proof that the Arab enmity toward the Jews does not date merely from the inception of the modern state of Israel, but is centuries old. ''If there had been no other reason for Zionism,'' they say, ''it would have had to be invented in order to bring the centuries-long oppression of the Jews of the Arab world to an end.'' (p. 169.)

3. There is much evidence in their own underground publications that they saw themselves as leaders of an armed revolution of the masses. It is apparent in Mahler's declaration in court, referred to in the article. Much more evidence can be found in *Über den bewaffneten Kampf in Westeuropa,* which was republished as *Rotbuch 29,* Verlag Klaus Wagenbach, Berlin, 1971, especially on pages 17, 19, 23, 46; *Das Konzept Stadtguerilla,* which was republished in *Stadtguerilla* by Alex Schubert, Verlag Klaus Wagenbach, Berlin, 1971, especially on pp. 109–16, 125; and *Dem Volk Dienen,* issued as an underground publication only. It will also be noticed in their own writings that they explicitly advocate the use of 'terror': see e.g. *Über den bewaffneten Kampf in Westeuropa,* section 6, *Terror gegen den Herrschaftsapparat—ein notwendiges Element der Massenkämpfe* (Terror against the Rulership Apparatus—a necessary element of the mass struggle), pp. 33–40. The last two sentences of the section read: ''The rulers use fear, which they produce through terror, to keep the proletariat compliant. So what can be said against the use of fear by the suppressed which they induce in their enemies through terror, so as to set themselves free at last?''

4. I have pointed out and discussed elsewhere the envy of victims and fascination with suffering in general (I call it *Leidensneid;* it is manifested, for instance, by the imitation of the appearance of poverty) among affluent young

radicals of the 1960s and 1970s. See Jillian Becker, *Hitler's Children,* Panther, Granada Publishing, London, 1977, 1978, pp. 69–71.

5. Ulrike Meinhof did not give an opinion as to whether the people were not guilty of the killing, enslavement, and persecution of any other races, Gypsies or Slavs for instance, to exonerate them from the charge of "racism" in general, only this ambiguous argument to clear them of "anti-Semitism." For a concise account of racism in the history of socialism, see George Watson, "Race and the Socialists," in *Encounter,* November 1976, in which he writes, for instance (pp. 20, 21): "Marx and Engels were not socialists who also happened to be racialists, or racialists who also happened to be socialists. They openly believed that the one conviction requires the other. . . . Equality (according to Marx and Engels) may be pursued—may have to be pursued—by killing those who are genetically unequal." The author also refers in his article to Ulrike Meinhof's statements at the trial of Horst Mahler, and asks, "How much was socialism, and how much national-socialism in her passionate self-defence?" (p. 23.)

6. Mahler's insistence that the developed countries are responsible for the poverty of the less developed, is widely held in the developed world. For a clear and impressive argument against it, backed by convincing facts, see Professor P.T. Bauer's "Western Guilt and Third World Poverty" in *Commentary,* New York, January 1976. Professor Bauer writes, for instance, ". . . allegations that the West is responsible for the poverty of the so-called Third World . . . have come to be widely accepted, often as axiomatic, yet they are not only untrue, but more nearly the opposite of the truth." (p. 31.). And again, "So far from the West having caused the poverty of the Third World, contact with the West has been the principal agent of material progress there." (p. 32.) He explains in the course of the article how Marxist-Leninist ideology reinforced mistaken notions which gave rise to the wide acceptance of the view that the West caused the poverty of the Third World. He further points out that, ". . . people in the West who are sufficiently disillusioned with their own society to have become disaffected from or even hostile to it . . . see the Third World as a useful instrument for promoting their cause in what is in essence a civil conflict in the West." (p. 38.)

7. It should be noted that during his years in prison, Horst Mahler has changed his mind about many of the views he held in the 1960s and early 1970s, and in particular has declared himself to be no longer in favor of terrorism.

8. Tom Wolfe in "The Me Decade and the Third Great Awakening," on p. 131 of *Mauve Gloves and Madmen, Clutter and Vine,* Bantam, London, 1977, writes: "It is entirely possible that in the long run historians will regard the entire New Left experience as not so much a political as a religious episode wrapped in semi-military gear and guerrilla talk."

9. Norman Cohn, *The Pursuit of the Millennium,* Paladin, London, 1970, p. 281.

10. The Angry Brigade was influenced by the French "Situationists." For the millenarian flavor of their political views, see e.g., Raoul Vaneigem, *The Revolution of Everyday Life,* Practical Paradise Publications, London, 1972.

11. But not all the millenarian groups which arose out of the New Left were "urban guerrilla" movements. There were—and still are—numerous cults, religions, and quasi-religions, of which many erstwhile supporters of the New Left became adherents. Some of these seem lunatic, exhibiting characteristics of such groups in an exaggerated form. One example was the Charles Manson "family," a drug-taking, murdering, orgiastic group, with weird but distinctly millenarian beliefs: a final war, between blacks and whites, which the blacks would win, though Manson ("Man's son," both "God and Satan," as he called himself) would then emerge from hiding in the desert of California, wrest victory from the blacks because they would find themselves simply unable to govern, and so establish his own blessed reign, a lasting peace on earth.

12. For details of their lives and characters, see Jillian Becker, op. cit., especially Parts One, Two, and Three.

13. Norman Cohn, op. cit., p. 217.

14. For instances of this, and their preference for high living standards and luxury goods, see Jillian Becker, op. cit., especially e.g., pp. 230, 245–46.

15. Norman Cohn, op. cit., p. 281. And on p. 282: "Revolutionary millenarianism drew its strength from a population living on the margins of society—peasants without land . . . beggars and vagabonds—in fact from the amorphous mass of people who were not simply poor but who could find no assured and recognised place in society at all." Cf. Herbert Marcuse, one of the Marxist philosophers most favored by the New Left, who writes in *One Dimensional Man,* Sphere Books, London, 1972, pp. 199–200, that the true revolutionaries now were not the working classes but "the substratum of the outcasts and outsiders . . . the unemployed and the unemployable." The Red Army Faction did not despair of leading the working classes too, but in fact they led neither the proletariat nor the *lumpenproletariat.*

16. Norman Cohn, op. cit., p. 245.

17. Ibid., p. 244.

18. Ibid., p. 255.

19. Ibid., p. 251.

20. Ibid., p. 120.

21. Ibid., p. 125.

22. I have said (in *Hitler's Children*) that the chief real motivation for these terrorists was ego gratification. Following the usage that Karl Popper prefers (see *The Open Society and Its Enemies,* Routledge and Kegan Paul, London,

1969, fifth edition, p. 101), I distinguish between "individualism" and "egoism." The individualist is *opposed* to collectivism. The egoist, by contrast, often seeks emotional satisfaction in membership of a group or tribe, as Popper explains. Furthermore, the Red Army Faction and similar terrorist groups selected individuals for attack and killing on the grounds that they were to be regarded primarily as representatives of groups—capitalists, managers, bankers, industrialists; judges, public prosecutors; shoppers in department stores; etc. As this is precisely equivalent to persecuting individuals on the grounds that they "represent" this or that national or racial group, one might hear the moral indignation they like to express over "nationalism" or "racism" (even without remarking Ulrike Meinhof's view of Auschwitz as the just deserts of *"Geldjuden"*) as having a hollow ring.

23. Norman Cohn, op. cit., p. 108.
24. Ibid., p. 109.

# The British Police and Terrorism

F.E.C. Gregory

University of Southampton

*Abstract*      The police response to terrorism in England, Wales, and Scotland is considered with special emphasis on the necessity for good police-public relations in a democratic state. Legal and organizational developments related to preventing terrorism are evaluated by reference to the traditional view of the police and the police functions in Britain. The idea of a ''third force'' and the role of the Army in support of the police are also considered. The conclusions lay stress on the complexities of countering terrorism in a democracy.

In the study of terrorism and the problem of police response in democratic states there is a tendency to put too much emphasis on tactics and equipment or special units. This tendency is understandable given the nature of the terrorists' challenge to society and the rule of law. However, it neglects the fact that if the democratic state is to resist the terrorists' challenge and remain a democracy it must retain a publicly acceptable police system.[1] This is well expressed in Sam Souryal's *Police Administration and Management.* Souryal points out that, ''What distinguishes police practices in free societies from those exercised in communist or fascist societies is basically the relationship between the system of criminal justice and the sub-system of police. In the latter societies, police agencies simply operate on the assumption that they are, in fact, the criminal justice system. . . . In free societies, police agencies are, and must always remain, a sub-system—a component of the criminal justice system. Police administration and practices must stem from the criminal justice system—the legitimate agency in charge of 'establishing justice and insuring domestic tranquility'.''[2]

In this article I intend to analyze the police response to terrorism in England, Wales, and Scotland (these regions of the United Kingdom are referred to as Britain in the article). With reference to Sam Souryal's definition of police practices in a free society it can be said that in Britain the law establishes the duties of the police. However, within broad limits and constraints of manpower and finance the chief officers of police (the Chief Constables and Metropolitan Police Commissioners) can develop what they consider to be the appropriate organizational method of executing their duties under the law. The specific focus of this article is on the effect of terrorism upon police methods and the related effects upon police-public relations. As Lord Shackleton said, in his review of the operation of the Prevention of Terrorism Acts of 1974 and 1976, "There is a delicate relationship between the resolution of an urgent problem by the introduction of new powers and the longer-term effects of such measures."[3]

In Britain great care has been taken in defining the function and nature of the police, especially in the creation of a distinct decentralized and normally unarmed civilian police system, which is unlike the military and national police systems found on the continent of Europe. This aspect of the British police system is clearly set out in P. J. Stead's chapter entitled, "The New Police," in D. H. Bayley's book, *Police and Society*. Although elements of the military organizational model were necessarily used in the command and control structure of the police, the Metropolitan Police Act of 1829, "contained a provision that would always distinguish the policeman from the soldier."[4] The "New Police" were to hold the ancient office of constable. Each man, having taken the oath of constable is an officer of the Crown performing his duties according to law. Unlike many of the continental policemen, the British constable is neither an officer of the municipal government nor of the central government. Moreover, each constable has an individual duty to uphold the law which transcends his duty to obey his superiors in the police service.

The concept behind the "New Police"[5] as it is present in the British police today cannot be taken for granted in view of the problems, such as terrorism, facing British society. This point has been stressed in a number of recent studies of the British police. Looking back over his long police career a former Metropolitan Police Commissioner, Sir Robert Mark, wrote, "I had moreover arrived at the cynical conclusion that no political party really wants an effective, honest police force unswervingly dedicated to impartiality in all matters. Not of course that any party would admit this. And most politicians would hasten to pay lip service to the general principle. But at moments of crisis, each wants the police to see their point of view as the right one. . . .''[6] In this context P. Evans *(The Police Revolution)*, in referring to public turbulence, political protest, and violence, notes that, ''The policeman, whose job is supposed to be essentially non-political, is caught in the middle, trying to maintain public tranquility, as the gap between government and sections of the public widens.''[7] He also later points out that, ''The Special Branch has a pretty good idea of the people who are likely to stir up trouble as a means of subversion. But agitators have appeal only if the message they preach strikes a chord in the hearts and minds of people with a grievance. The means of removing that grievance do not lie within the powers of the police. The means are political.''[8] This point is also made by Ben Whitaker in *The Police in Society*. He writes, ''The one certainty is that growing awareness of, and refusal to accept, contradictions and inequalities in national and international society is liable to make the police's role of trying to preserve stability even harder.''[9]

Terrorist campaigns and riots pose a special organizational problem for the British Police because when the ''New Police'' were formed no provision was made for a special emergency reserve or a police intelligence service. As P. J. Stead points out, ''The English policeman, therefore, ever since the formation of the 'New Police,' has had to reconcile in his one person two very diverse roles: the role of the individually responsible and decisive constable, and the role of the disciplined, obedient member of a formation under command.''[10] In recent years it has become necessary, because of major public order problems, the growth of armed and organized crime as well as terrorism, to create permanent special emergency units and reserves rather than rely on the ordinary divisional policeman. It has also been necessary to expand the role of the police intelligence service, the Special Branch. These developments have raised fears in the country that a ''third force'' or form of paramilitary police might be evolving and fears have also been expressed about the surveillance, by the police, of various political and protest groups.

The idea of a ''third force'' is often mentioned when a state is facing either prolonged civil disorders or a terrorist campaign. It is contended that, when the ordinary police are being hard pressed and yet the breakdown of law and order is not such that martial law and the armed forces should take over, some form of paramilitary police may be able to help restore order. In fact, a true "third force" that is neither part of a police system nor an army unit is quite a rare organization. The CRS in France is often cited as an example of a "third force" but the CRS is an integral part of the Police Nationale. Similarly, the *carabinieri* in Italy is a unit of the Italian Army which for historical reasons also performs civilian police functions. The only Western European example of a "third force" is the West German Bundesgrenzschutz (the Federal Border Guard). The Bundesgrenzschutz is neither a unit of the West German Army nor part of the Länder police system. It is an independent force under the Federal Minister of the Interior.

A British police view of the ideal roles of the police, the armed forces, and the citizens linked to the idea of a "third force" was well expressed by Mr. J. C. Alderson when he was Commandant of the Police College in 1973. Mr. Alderson was addressing the Royal United Services Institute on the theme, "The Role of the Police in Society." In his lecture Mr. Alderson said that the Army should not be involved in keeping the peace in England. However, he felt that the Army did have a role in helping the police deal with armed terrorists. He was asked, "If there is such a requirement, should not the police themselves be raising and equipping a force to deal with that situation rather than getting the Army involved?" Mr. Alderson replied, "If you are getting the idea of the gendarmes, the third force between the police and the Army, I always say that the police in this country are the third force, with the first being the public and the second being the Army."[11]

Mr. Alderson was referring to the historical relationship between the citizen, the Army, and the Police. In this relationship the citizen had most of the powers and duties of a policeman and the army was only to be called in when the citizenry could not cope with public order problems. Thus the introduction of the "New Police" could be viewed as providing a "third force." However, to the public a "third force" may seem to have developed where the police forces find it necessary to depart from the familiar methods of divisional policing and establish special units under central control.

In the context of the preceding discussion of the origins of the British police system and its position in contemporary British society I intend now to examine the particular problems posed for the police forces in Britain by the type of terrorist campaigns and incidents that England, Wales, and Scotland have so far faced. These can be partly described by reference to Paul Wilkinson's category of "spasm" terrorism which he describes as a "series of attacks of relatively low intensity and brief duration."[12] In addition, the police may always have to deal with an isolated and ad hoc terrorist incident.

Terrorism in the United Kingdom has produced three additions to the law and hence additions to the duties and powers of the police. These are the Prevention of Terrorism Acts of 1974 and 1976 and the Policing of Airports Act 1974.[13] The Prevention of Terrorism Act is of limited duration and must be renewed by the order of the Home Secretary. The 1974 Act contained the following provisions: The Home Secretary can proscribe an organization as illegal (so far only the IRA and the Irish National Liberation Army have been proscribed); the authorities can exclude persons from entry to the country in order to prevent terrorism; the police may arrest without warrant for offenses under the Act and they may detain suspects for 48 hours and for a further 5 days with the Home Secretary's approval. Under the 1976 Act these provisions were supplemented by powers to exclude persons specifically from Northern Ireland; by creating a new offense of withholding without reasonable excuse information relating to terrorism, and the offense of supporting terrorist activities was broadened in its scope.

Lord Shackleton said in his review of the operation of these Acts: "I can conclude by reference to the truism that basic civil liberties include the rights to stay alive and to go about one's business without fear. A society will always seek to defend itself against threats to its security." He also described the implications of the Acts for the police in that, "Society expects the police rapidly and effectively to detect and prevent acts of terrorism; the police may sometimes feel, however, that their room for manoeuvre is limited. They know that whenever they use these powers they will face criticism in some quarters . . . but they also know they are equally open to criticism if they fail to prevent acts of terrorism."[14]

Because of the international nature of contemporary terrorism one cannot omit, from the legal background for British police operations, obligations created by international agreements and in particular those affecting the Western European states. In August 1978 the European Convention on the Suppression of Terrorism came into force. It was signed by 17 out of the 19 members of the Council of Europe. Malta and Ireland were the two nonsignatory states. The Convention basically aims to reduce the opportunities for terrorists to escape prosecution by going out of the country where they have committed an offense, such as attacking a diplomat. Some members of the EEC were unhappy with the provisions of this Convention and in consequence the EEC Ministers of Justice drafted a European Community Convention on Terrorism. The European Community Convention gives more scope for the member states to decide if extradition can be refused on grounds of the political nature of an offense.

At present the governments of the EEC countries encourage their police forces to cooperate in antiterrorist work by exchanging information about terrorists and the methods of handling terrorist incidents. France, in the context of the negotiations on the Community Terrorism Convention, has proposed a higher level of community action in crime fighting, namely, the development of a common legal code.[15] If the implications of a community legal code will include changes in the British criminal justice system, making it more like some continental legal systems and even their police systems then these would be vigorously resisted by the British police and probably by the government of the day.[16] This potential issue further underlines the point that all antiterrorist efforts must be acceptable to the nation as a whole.

Having briefly considered the legal background, I am now going to define the functions required of the British police in response to the existence of terrorist threats as: intelligence gathering; prevention of and protection against terrorist acts and the ability to carry out counterterrorist operations. As Paul Wilkinson has noted, these tasks are "closely analogous to those required for combating other serious crimes of violence. But the tasks involved require a high degree of specialized knowledge and experience combined with tactics, techniques and intelligence resources beyond the scope of normal criminal investigation departments."[17]

The task of gathering intelligence related to terrorist groups and their activities is the primary responsibility of a group of plain-clothes officers known as the Special Branch. The Special Branch came into existence in 1883 as a response to the Irish terrorist movements of that period and until 1961 the Special Branch existed only as part of the Metropolitan Police. Since 1961 regional Special Branch Squads have been established. In the regional forces, the Special Branch officers are responsible to their Chief Constable for their activities. In the Metropolitan Police, the Special Branch, and the Anti-Terrorist Squad, are responsible to the Commissioner through the Assistant Commissioner (Crime).[18] The duties of the Special Branch are defined as the investigation of subversive or terrorist organizations; concern with offenses against the security of the state (e.g., espionage and treason); and offenses against the Official Secrets Act and the Public Order Act. The Special Branch also makes inquiries concerning aliens and watch persons entering the country via ports and airports.[19]

The overall size of the Special Branch has increased from around 200 just after World War II to over 1,000 today. In May 1978 the then Home Secretary, Mr. M. Rees, gave the House of Commons the first official figures made public since the 1920s of the officers in or attached to the Special Branch. In 1978 the Metropolitan Police had 409 Special Branch officers and the regional forces in England and Wales had 850 Special Branch officers.[20] Of the latter figure some 300 officers outside London are assigned to ports. There are a further 120 Special Branch officers in Scotland; of this number 61 are in the Strathclyde force and 21 in the Lothian and Borders force.[21]

The majority of the public are either unaware of or unconcerned about the activities of the Special Branch, but people concerned with civil liberties and the rights of the individual have raised a number of valid points about police intelligence work. First, there has been an unnecessary amount of official reticence about giving even general information concerning the Special Branch. Mr. Robin Cook, MP, noted in a Commons debate that of 36 Chief Constables' annual reports for 1977, made available to the Commons, only one report (from Durham) actually mentioned the Special Branch. The Commissioner of the Metropolitan Police did not mention his Special Branch until the 1978 report. Hopefully, Mr. Rees, when Home Secretary, set a precedent for succeeding Home Secretaries to at least allow the Special Branch to be discussed in a reasonably informative manner.

The other two main issues related to the work of the Special Branch are linked; the issues are: how the work of the Special Branch is officially defined and the consequences for the public of its defined tasks. The information-gathering work of the Special Branch relating to terrorist activities is obviously designed to preserve the internal security of the country and its system of government against what is generally called "subversion." However, there is no one official definition of "subversion." Lord Denning in his report on the Profumo case in 1963 defined subversion as being the acts of those who "would contemplate the overthrow of the Government by unlawful means."[22] This was a definition which carefully related subversion to attempts to break the law.

Since then, Home Office Ministers have considerably broadened the definition of subversion and hence the official scope of Special Branch activity. In 1975, Lord Harris, Minister of State at the Home Office, defined subversion as "activities which threaten the safety or well being of the state and are intended to undermine or overthrow parliamentary democracy by political, industrial or violent means,"[23] and this definition was repeated by the then Home Secretary Mr. M. Rees in April 1978.[24] However, Mr. Rees had also suggested a very broad role for the Special Branch when he had told the Commons only a month before that, "The Special Branch collects information on those who I think cause problems for the State."[25] Such a statement has unfortunate connotations as it implies a personal view rather than an agreed government policy on subversion.

It is the criteria for the collection of information that are of the greatest concern to the civil liberties lobby. Also, there is no opportunity for Parliament to debate an annual report on the Special Branch and this country does not have any means to enable citizens to find out if and why they may be in police records even if they have never been charged with a criminal offense. According to some civil liberties writers, a police "national computer," operating since 1974, contained by December 1977 records of 3.8 million people but records of only 2.2 million fingerprints,[26] suggesting that 1.6 million people are on file although they have never actually been charged with a criminal offense. The civil liberties writers do not cite a source for their figures. According to a press report in 1978 by *The Times* crime reporter Stewart Tendler, the police have been discussing, under Home Office auspices, a national police intelligence system which would probably concentrate on such matters as drugs, large-scale fraud, and terrorism. However, this report suggested that the police were not then contemplating using any form of national computer system because of public anxiety about computerized records.[27] In this context a restraint on computerized records does not apply to the use of the Metropolitan Police's new criminal intelligence computer. The Home Secretary has told the Commons that space is available to the Special Branch on this computer.[28] Little hard information on this important matter is available although the White Paper, *Computers: Safeguards For Privacy*, did state that the computer would handle, "information held by the Metropolitan Police about crime, criminals and their associates. The system will be internal to those branches of the force who now use this information in manually held records and it will not be connected to any other system."[29]

Recently, this whole issue of the nature of information kept about citizens came to the fore and in a way closely related to the discussion in this article. At the Old Bailey, four people were on trial for offenses such as unlawful possession of firearms and explosive substances, and the prosecution alleged that the discovery of the arms and ammunition "is clearly part of a picture of arming for terrorism."[30] At the start of the trial the *Guardian* newspaper published information suggesting that the original panel of jurors had been vetted. One potential juror, challenged by the Crown, was an old Etonian and a Professor of Finance and Accounting who claimed that the only time he had publicly protested was about not being able to buy gold from the Bank of England.

Roy Lewis has pointed out that, "The Special Branch has no special powers beyond those of ordinary policemen, of which it is composed. . . . It is demonstrably puny when compared with the resources available to police states like Russia or East Germany."[31] However, if a democratic society like Britain is to have a publicly acceptable police intelligence branch to counter terrorist threats, then some official action is necessary to emphasize police accountability in this area of work. Although it is generally accepted that the secret services, with one of which, M15, the Special Branch has a close liaison, must remain secret to be effective, it does not seem unreasonable that some attempt be made to draw up clear official guidelines for the work of the Special Branch which, together with some information about its organization and even achievements, could be reported to Parliament by the Home Secretary. In this context, the "Special Branch (Accountability) Adjournment Debate" held in the Commons in May 1978 provides a precedent.

In Britain the task of preventing and protecting against terrorist acts is the responsibility of the ordinary police, the police of government departments and other statutory bodies, and the Army, the latter operating under police control. The police duties in this context can best be understood if they are divided into the following tasks: The guarding of buildings, such as an embassy, or the guarding of a complex of buildings, such as an airport or an atomic energy establishment; the protection of persons by the provision of bodyguards and the provision of extra manpower to support the divisional police or a regional force in an area where terrorists are believed to be active.

With regard to the first task and the large number of terrorist incidents involving attacks on aircraft and at airports that have occurred throughout the world, it is not surprising that the British Police have assumed a larger role at airports in recent years. Under the Policing of Airports Acts 1974 the Metropolitan Police took over responsibility for policing Heathrow Airport from the British Airports Authority Police. Other local forces are taking similar responsibilities at Britain's other major airports, e.g., the Sussex Police are responsible for policing Gatwick Airport. The task of airport protection is shared with the armed forces where effective preventive policing requires the availability of an armed response that properly belongs to the armed forces, e.g., the use of armored vehicles. Large-scale military and police exercises were held at Heathrow Airport in 1973 and at Edinburgh Airport in 1978. The usual format for such cooperation is for the Army's specialist antiterrorist unit, the Special Air Services Regiment (SAS), to provide small "commando" units inside the airport while other Army units, such as an armored regiment, provide perimeter defense.

Complexes such as Ministry of Defense Establishments and the establishments of the Atomic Energy Authority and other public bodies are protected by these bodies' own police forces. These forces are sanctioned by Act of Parliament, and all the personnel are Special Constables. The strength of all these forces is about 15,000.[32] One of these forces, the Atomic Energy Authority Police, has received special powers because of the possible consequences of terrorist acts against nuclear installations. Under the Atomic Energy Authority (Special Constables) Act 1976 this force was permitted to carry arms and its area of authority was extended from an area within a 15-mile radius of AEA property to anywhere where AEA property is either in storage or in transit. Also, an AEA police officer may exercise the powers of a constable to pursue, arrest, or place in custody a person or persons anywhere when necessary on reasonable grounds, such as unlawfully removing or attempting to remove nuclear materials from the Crown, AEA, a specified corporate body, or a designated company.[33]

The arming of the AEA Police, although a reasonable precaution against terrorist attacks on nuclear installations, was criticized on grounds of the lack of accountability of the AEA Police, "Justice," the British section of the International Commission of Jurists, said to the Windscale Inquiry that British "Police forces, who are generally not armed with firearms, certainly not automatic ones, are answerable to elected police authorities. By contrast the chief constable of the AEA's special constabulary is answerable only to that authority, which is an appointed not elected body. We view with some concern the creation of a constitutionally unique armed force of this kind, however desirable its existence and equipment may be in the interests of security. Its structure conflicts with all our traditions of civilian and politically accountable policing."[34] However, it should be noted that the AEA police officers as Special Constables are individually accountable in law for their actions.

Embassies, being located in London, are the responsibility of the Metropolitan Police and they are guarded by a special police unit, the Diplomatic Protection Group. This group "provides permanent surveillance of embassies and private residences with mobile patrols and is comprised of volunteers who serve for periods of six months. About a third of the group are permanently armed."[35] The Metropolitan Police provides additional personal protection services from its Royalty Protection Group and the Special Branch. Recently a Deputy Assistant Commissioner of the Metropolitan Police was appointed as coordinator of all the units concerned with protection duties, the Royalty Protection Group, the Diplomatic Protection Group, and the Special Branch.[36]

The provision of extra manpower to support divisional or regional forces in antiterrorist duties can best be considered by reference to the nature of the support provided. Support may be permanent or ad hoc, and it may comprise specialist or nonspecialist manpower. The nature of the support will depend upon the immediacy of the actual or potential terrorist problem and the police manpower available. In general, the police forces in large urban areas have available a mobile reserve section which can help the divisional police with such problems as crowd control, major crime investigations, and antiterrorist operations. The

Metropolitan Police has the ca. 200-strong Special Patrol Group, Birmingham had a similarly named unit, and Bristol has formed a Special Services Squad. These mobile reserves are necessary and useful to help the divisional police but they do mark an innovation in British police organization. Perhaps the major difficulty arises from the nature of some of their duties when the public may come to consider them as the "riot squad" or the "tough squad." As P. Evans has pointed out, "no group of officers from a central organization can have the same sensitive awareness of the local situation as the local policemen."[37]

Given either a permanently available or ad hoc police reserve, the next requirement for effective antiterrorist operations is a specialist squad or squads. In the Metropolitan Police area the specialist squad is the Anti-terrorist Squad which was formed in 1976 from the Metropolitan Police's Bomb Squad. The Squad has a strength of about 140 officers. In antiterrorist operations the Anti-terrorist Squad can receive support from the squad of expert marksmen, D 11, and the Technical Support Branch, which provides listening and surveillance devices.[38] Outside the London area, the regional forces tend to create "anti-terrorist squads" when they are required. For example, in response to the bombing campaign in the Birmingham area in 1973–74 the Birmingham Police created a Bomb Squad of ca. 100 men out of their Serious Crimes Squad.[39] All the police squads that may be concerned with bombing incidents can obtain specialist help from the Army Bomb Disposal Squads to deal with explosive devices. The police are also assisted in identifying the explosives and detonation methods by the Home Office explosive experts working at the Royal Armament Research and Development Establishment.

The actual conduct of antiterrorist operations can pose a delicate problem for the police, namely, when and how to call on the Army for support. In this context, Army support does not include the use of the Army Bomb Disposal teams. Such help is of a routine nature and has a long history. The problem for the police arises when Army combat units are required to assist the police in operations where military training equipment and tactics are necessary. As Ben Whitaker points out, "the use of the army for policing has always been unpopular in Britain since Cromwell's time. . . ."[40] Sir Robert Mark, when Metropolitan Police Commissioner, stated clearly in 1976 that the functions of the civil police and the Army were wholly separate. He stated that, except for civil emergencies, the police only needed Army assistance in such instances as antiterrorist operations at an airport.[41] In practice, the division of responsibility seems to rest upon tactical considerations of the nature of the terrorist problem and the response required in terms of training and weaponry. The principal Army antiterrorist unit is the 22 SAS Regiment which has "anti-terrorist units, wearing plain clothes and using Range Rovers and Rover 3500 cars, on permanent three-minute standby. . . . "[42] If, as appears the case at airports, additional uniformed Army units are required, then these can be drawn from any available infantry or armored units.

Therefore, for the conduct of antiterrorist operations the police in England, Scotland, and Wales very much regard themselves as being the proper and principal source of expertise and manpower. A good example of a police antiterrorist operation was the siege of five IRA gunmen with their hostages in Balcombe Street in London in 1975. In this operation the mobile manpower reserve, the Special Patrol Group, provided the area police cordon while members of the, then, Bomb Squad were aided by D 11, the marksmen, and the Technical Support Branch.

The British policy of relying principally on the civil police for antiterrorist work is excellent as it is a most acceptable form of response to terrorist threats in a democratic society. However, it does contain an inherent dilemma. If there was a prolonged increase in terrorist activities, what would be the response? The police could develop more military style antiterrorist units, perhaps on the pattern of the special units of the West German Federal Border Guard. Alternatively, the Army could become more involved in antiterrorist operations.

Apart from the issue of the acceptability of the response to the government of the day it is particularly important that the response should be acceptable to *both* the public and the police, since the police function in a democracy rests essentially upon the consent of the citizen to be policed. Roy Lewis in his discussion of mobile squads and third-force ideas suggests that the public may in fact be reassured by police preparations for such things as terrorism. He contends that, "it is quite likely that the wider public would be reassured rather than dismayed, preferring the police to show signs of forethought. Most people were not shocked by the police marksmen on whom television cameras dwelt so lovingly during the Balcombe Street siege."[43] By way of contrast, Ben Whitaker cites the following comment of a Chief Constable: "Did the heavy involvement of the military in Northern Ireland produce the present situation or did it prevent something worse? We have seen in other parts of the world that the involvement of the military can lead to a crystallization of affairs with a stalemate, no progress one way or the other. Paradoxically sometimes a weak police force causes society to come to terms with its problems and take political action which it would be discouraged from doing if the security services were strong.'"[44]

In this article I have examined the response of the police in England, Scotland, and Wales to the challenge of "spasm terrorism." In so doing I have considered the organizational changes that have occurred together with any issues that these changes have raised for the traditional British approach to the police function. My conclusions are necessarily related, first, to such important factors as the level of popular support for government policies and the effects of domestic social and economic problems. Second, my conclusions are related to the consequences of these factors for the police both in organizational and operational terms; for example, do the police at a given time enjoy a good measure of government and public support? Are the police adequately paid? How acute is their manpower shortage? Third, my conclusions must consider the nature of the terrorist threat. If the terrorist campaign arises because of the neglect of a domestic problem, then the primary response should come from the government. In this case the government may be able to tackle the domestic problem in such a way that the terrorists no longer have a cause. However, if terrorist violence is used either as an alternative to the normal democratic political processes in order to gain domestic political power or to bring pressure on Britain over an external issue, such as the Palestine cause, then the primary response must come from the police, and be publicly acceptable. In this respect I suggest that terrorism poses the following general problems for the police and the government.

The counterterrorist intelligence-gathering requirement is fulfilled under official guidelines, as to who or what organizations should be under surveillance, these guidelines being apparently couched in very general terms, and citizens are sometimes amazed at the scope of the domestic intelligence operations of the Special Branch. In this area it seems necessary that there be less official reticence and more clarity concerning the work of the Special Branch so that Parliament and the public can better appreciate the importance of intelligence gathering in successful antiterrorist work.

In order that the police can prevent terrorist acts or protect the public against them it has been necessary for the police to develop specialist units of policemen with expertise in such fields as crowd control, the use of firearms, surveillance techniques, and the complexities of negotiating with persons holding hostages. Unfortunately, these developments, which have taken place on an essentially ad hoc basis, have changed the traditional form of unarmed policing which relied upon the policeman being a sort of "generalist" in terms of police work. Mr. James Anderton, the Chief Constable of Greater Manchester, recently commented that his 72-strong Tactical Aid Group was not a "tough, hard-hitting, paramilitary force" and that "the public has nothing to fear from a group of well-trained police officers whose purpose in life is fully understood and appreciated, that is the best protection and security of the public."[45] I would entirely agree with Mr. Anderton's comments but I suggest that in fact the public does not always understand the necessity for, or the function of, such police units.

The conduct of actual operations against terrorists raises the issue of police-army relations and their respective roles in antiterrorist operations. This again is an area where perhaps official unwillingness to discuss the functions and relations of the Army and the police can cause unnecessary public anxiety.

Britain has evolved what Norman Fowler has described as a "cautious stance" in its response to terrorism, where "[t]he police have a limited armed role but not so pronounced as to interfere with their reputation as a civil force serving the community."[46] However, as Sir Robert Mark has admitted, the response to terrorism has been surrounded by "needless secrecy" which is more likely "to provoke than allay social disquiet."[47]

## References

1. These issues were first examined by the author in "Protest and Violence: the Police Response," *Conflict Study No. 75* (London: Institute for the Study of Conflict, 1976).

2. S. S. Souryal, *Police Administration and Management* (St. Paul, Minn.: West Pub. Co., 1977), pp. 79–80.

3. The Rt. Hon. Lord Shackleton, KG, OBE, *Review of the operation of the Prevention*

*of Terrorism (Temporary Provisions) Acts of 1974 and 1976.* (London: HMSO, Cmnd 7324, 1978), p. 48.

4.  P. J. Stead, "The New Police," in D. H. Bayley (Ed.), *Police and Society* (London: Sage, 1977), pp. 79–80.

5.  A summary of the traditional views of the founding of the "New Police" is contained in C. D. Robinson, "Ideology as History: A Look at the Way Some English Police Historians Look at the Police," *Police Studies,* Vol. 2 (1979), pp. 35–47. These views may be contrasted with the view of the British Police as an instrument of working-class oppression found in T. Bunyan, *The Political Police in Britain* (London: Quartet Books, 1977).

6.  Sir Robert Mark, GBE, QPM, *In the Office of Constable* (London: Collins, 1978), p. 240.

7.  P. Evans, *The Police Revolution* (London: Allen & Unwin, 1976), p. 42.

8.  Ibid., p. 127.

9.  B. Whitaker, *The Police in Society* (London: Eyre Methuen: 1979), p. 15.

10. P. J. Stead, op. cit., pp. 82–83.

11. J. C. Alderson, Esq., Commandant of the Police College, Bramshill, "The Role of the Police in Society," *R U S I Journal,* Vol. 118, No. 4 (1973), pp. 18–23.

12. P. Wilkinson, *Terrorism and the Liberal State* (London: Macmillan, 1977), p. 139.

13. The full titles of the Terrorism Acts are *The Prevention of Terrorism (Temporary Provisions) Acts* of 1974 and 1976. It must be noted that there is a slight variation of police duties and powers in Scotland, which has a separate legal system. The *Policing of Airports Act 1974* allows the Home Secretary, for the preservation of peace and the prevention of crime, to make orders designating that a civil aerodrome be policed by the local police and not the police maintained by an airport authority.

14. Lord Shackleton, op. cit., pp. 48–49.

15. The French position on this issue was recently stated by the French Foreign Minister and reported in *The Guardian,* October 22, 1979. A general discussion of European Community cooperation against crime is contained in R. Lewis, *A Force for the Future* (London: Temple Smith, 1976), pp. 235–36.

16. Strong defenses of the British police system have been made with references to continental police systems and ideas about a national police force. See, e.g., N. Fowler, *After the Riots: the Police in Europe* (London: Davis-Poynter, 1979), pp. 68–82; a speech by Sir Robert Mark in London as reported in *The Times,* June 23, 1977, and a lecture by the Chief Constable of Devon and Cornwall, Mr. John Alderson, reported in *The Times,* May 4, 1977. Moreover, on a specific issue the present Metropolitan Police Commissioner, Sir David McNee, stated bluntly, "there is no similarity between my SPG, which is basically a crime fighting unit and the French CRS." Sir David's remarks were reported in *The Daily Telegraph,* May 23, 1979.

17. P. Wilkinson, op. cit., p. 140.

18. For accounts of the Special Branch, see *Report to the Home Secretary from the Commissioner of Police of the Metropolis on the Actions of Police Officers concerned with the case of Kenneth Joseph Lennon.* (London: HMSO, H. C. 351,

1974); T. Bunyan, op. cit., pp. 102–50; R. Lewis, op. cit., pp. 115–18, and B. Whitaker, op. cit., pp. 198–200.

19. This definition of the duties of the Special Branch is taken from *Lord Denning's Report* (London: HMSO, Cmnd, 2152, 1963), p. 25.
20. See the statement by Mr. Rees in the "Special Branch (Accountability) Adjournment Debate," *950 HC Debs. 5s*, Col. 1718–19, May 24, 1978.
21. The figures for Scotland are taken from B. Whitaker, op. cit., p. 199.
22. *Lord Denning's Report,* op. cit., p. 77.
23. Lord Harris's definition is cited in B. Whitaker, op. cit., p. 198.
24. *947 HC Debs 5s.,* Col. 618, April 6, 1978.
25. *945 HC Debs 5s.,* Col. 650, March 2, 1978.
26. P. Hain (Ed.) with D. Humphrey and B. Rose-Smith, *Policing the Police* (London: John Calder, 1979), p. 19.
27. *The Times,* May 9, 1978.
28. *Weekly Hansard,* No. 1136, March 23–29, 1979, Col. 608.
29. *Computers: Safeguards for Privacy* (London: HMSO Cmnd. 6354, 1975), pp. 29–31.
30. Address of Mr. M. Worsley, prosecuting counsel, as reported in *The Daily Telegraph,* September 28, 1979.
31. R. Lewis, op. cit., p. 116.
32. Ibid., p. 40.
33. The original restrictions on the authority of the AEA constables were contained in the *Nuclear Installations Act 1965.*
34. Statement for "Justice" by Mr. Paul Sieghart, barrister, to the Windscale Inquiry, Oct. 10, 1977, as reported in *The Times,* October 11, 1977.
35. T. Bunyan, op. cit., p. 95.
36. Report of the appointment of DAC David Helm to the post of coordinator in *The Daily Telegraph,* October 5, 1979.
37. P. Evans, op. cit., p. 156, and see the discussion on the role of the Metropolitan Police SPG in Lord Justice Scarman's inquiry, *The Red Lion Square Disorders of 15 June 1974* (London: HMSO, Cmnd. 5919, 1975).
38. Useful sources on the British police antiterrorist squads and tactics are T. Bowden, "Men in the Middle—the UK Police," *Conflict Study No. 68* (London: Institute for the Study of Conflict, 1976), pp. 14–15, and N. Fowler, op. cit., pp. 108–20.
39. B. Gibson, *The Birmingham Bombs* (London: Barry Rose, 1976), pp. 8–21.
40. B. Whitaker, op. cit., p. 51.
41. Sir Robert Mark's statement is paraphrased in R. Lewis, op. cit., p. 282.
42. B. Whitaker, op. cit., p. 51.
43. R. Lewis, op. cit., p. 283.
44. B. Whitaker, op. cit., p. 51.
45. Mr. Anderton's Address to a SSAFA forum at Southport was reported in *The Daily Telegraph,* October 15, 1979.
46. N. Fowler, op. cit., p. 118.
47. Sir Robert Mark's comments were cited in *The Times,* March 12, 1976.

# Management of the Kidnap Risk

Richard Clutterbuck

University of Exeter

*Abstract*      Paradoxically, Britain, where kidnapping is rare, has been a pioneer in kidnap insurance, prevention, and negotiation, largely due to the experience of Lloyd's of London in underwriting every kind of risk worldwide. The premium income of Lloyd's for kidnap insurance has grown from $150,000 in 1970 to $50 million in 1976. As with fire risks, with kidnap risks Lloyd's found that it saved money both for the underwriters and their clients if they sent specialist consultants to advise on reducing the risk and, in the event of a kidnap, to advise on negotiation. A firm at Lloyd's founded such a consultancy (Control Risks Ltd.) which has now expanded to meet a rising demand, not only from insured clients, but also from an increasing number of uninsured clients who engage them on a consultancy fee basis. This article examines the growing attractiveness of kidnapping as a high-yield low-risk crime (whether for political dividends or criminal gain); describes how kidnaps are organized; advises on the various means of protection against it; and discusses the acts of contingency planning and crisis management if a kidnap occurs.

It may seem surprising that Great Britain, where kidnapping has been very rare, should have been a pioneer in developing the techniques of protection and insurance against it as well as in the art of negotiating for the release of hostages. There are two reasons for this: the historic necessity for Britain of maintaining overseas trade has for centuries exposed British businessmen to the risks of operating as individuals in distant and lawless lands; and, linked to this, Britain's long maritime predominance resulted in the evolution of Lloyd's of London as the leaders in the world's insurance market, covering every kind of risk.

As examples of this continuing threat, three British businessmen, with the wife and child of one of them, were the victims of sensational overseas kidnappings in 1978–79. Two executives of Lloyds Bank International were kidnapped in El Salvador in November 1978 and held hostage for seven months; and in August 1979 Rolf Schild was kidnapped in Sardinia with his wife and daughter.

## The Lloyd's Initiative

Lloyd's underwriters (no connection, incidentally, with Lloyds Bank—note the apostrophe!) have covered piracy and ransom in their maritime policies for over two centuries, but there have been two hinge years in the development of kidnap and ransom insurance: in 1933 the kidnapping and murder of the Lindbergh baby triggered a demand for insurance; and in 1971 a sudden burgeoning of kidnappings of bankers and their families in the United States and of diplomats and expatriate executives in Argentina caused a spectacular growth in this demand. In 1970, Lloyd's kidnap and ransom premium income was $150,000. It is reported that in 1976 Lloyd's had a $50 million share of a worldwide gross annual premium income of $70 million.[1]

Kidnapping for ransom has been highly profitable both for political terrorists and criminal gangs. The largest recorded ransom was $60 million paid for the release in 1974 of the two sons of the president of Argentina's largest firm, Bunge Born. This was paid to the Peronist guerrilla movement, the Montoneros, who amassed $240 million in ransoms in less than three years. More recently, political terrorists in El Salvador are said to have raised $50 million in two years (1978–79). In Italy, the great majority of kidnappings have been carried out by criminal gangs, who have found it a high-yield low-risk crime, better than bank robbery, and are estimated to have extorted $200 million (frequently by kidnapping children) in the last ten years.[2]

The Italian government has attempted to deter the payment of ransoms by banning kidnap insurance inside Italy or (occasionally) by freezing the assets of the victim or his family. The result, however, has been a dismally low rate of arrests and convictions, largely because the restriction on their freedom of action has driven desperate fathers or wives to settle behind the backs of the police.

The commonest arguments against kidnap insurance are that if the kidnappers know that the victim is insured they may demand a bigger ransom; that they may believe that his family or firm may be more ready to pay; and that they may pay more quickly. In fact, however, since secrecy is a condition of such insurance, there has been only one known case in which there was evidence that the kidnappers did know. A girl who had previously worked for the victim in a confidential capacity had joined the gang which kidnapped him. That was five years ago. There have been no known cases since in which there was any evidence to suggest that the kidnappers knew that the victim was insured.

In practice, when a potential victim or his firm is insured, this should reduce the likelihood of his selection as a target because the responsible underwriters insist upon—and contribute to—the taking of better precautions to prevent it. Few people would doubt that fire insurance reduces the risk of fire and theft insurance reduces the risk of burglary. Kidnappers, like thieves, will always look for the easier target and the underwriters will make sure that those they cover are *not* easy targets. In Italy, for example, where many firms and families are insured, not a single one of the 70 kidnappings reported in 1979 was of a client insured at Lloyd's.

Lloyd's do not themselves pay ransoms; they write only policies of reimbursement. The client has to pay from his own resources and they limit the policy to the amount they judge he would be able to pay. Before they reimburse the client, Lloyd's send their assessors (as with fire and other kinds of insurance) to satisfy themselves that there has been no fraud or collusion and that the conditions of the policy have been met.

The conditions of a Lloyd's policy include a requirement that, if a kidnap occurs, the client notifies the police and cooperates with them. There is always a similar condition in every theft policy. The prospect of a quick panic settlement behind the backs of the police is the greatest attraction to kidnappers, while the prospect of a hue and cry and subsequent conviction is the greatest deterrent.

Another condition is that the policy is kept secret from everyone but an agreed list of those who need to know. It is now a common practice for multinational companies to cover all executives and staff whom they consider to be at risk without the individuals ever knowing that they are covered at all.

## Surveyors and Consultants

The man who conceived the idea of a specialist consultancy was Julian Radcliffe, a young executive then aged 26, of a leading firm of brokers at Lloyd's. There is a historic parallel in that it was the insurance companies in Britain which pioneered both fire surveyors and fire fighting brigades. It was in the interests of both the insurers and the insured that the risk of fire should be reduced and that, should it occur, the cost of damage should be minimized.

So with kidnap insurance. Radcliffe offered to provide the underwriters with an independent team of specialist surveyors who would visit the client before the attachment of the insurance, to assess the risk and advise on reducing it. The underwriters contribute towards the surveyor's fees and if the client acts upon his advice the premium may be reduced—as is also the standard practice with fire insurance.

If a kidnap occurs, a consultant from Control Risks, possibly the man who did the survey, will fly out at once to the scene to advise on crisis management and negotiation, again at the underwriter's expense.

Control Risks have expanded rapidly to meet the rising demand. By the end of 1978 they had nine consultants. Many of them were officers finishing tours of duty with the Special Air Service (SAS), the elite British army unit which has, among other things, special responsibilities for intelligence and for the security of British VIPs (such as ambassadors) in high-risk areas. By the end of 1979 Control Risks had over 20 consultants backed by a London-based staff including an information center which maintained up-to-date country profiles, with data about the threat from both criminal and political groups, and about economic, political, and social conditions.

By 1980 the total staff exceeded 50. They had conducted surveys for corporations or individuals in 43 countries and had advised during post-kidnap negotiations in over 50 cases. Of the victims in these cases one was killed during an attempted rescue by the local police; one was murdered by his captors; one is missing, presumed dead; all the others were released safely, after the ransom had been greatly reduced.

Among the results of this rapid growth in demand for their service has been the great increase in the number of clients who are not insured but who engage Control Risks—both for surveys and post-kidnap consultancy—on a normal daily fee basis. Many large firms for whom they have done surveys now pay them a retainer in exchange for a guarantee that a consultant will fly out immediately in the event of a kidnap to advise on crisis management and negotiation.

During his survey, the consultant will also have advised the client and his firm, family, or lawyer on their crisis management plan, so the survey recommendations and the professional advice before and after the kidnap are likely to ensure that the client does not make a panic settlement.[3]

Full cooperation between the police and the victim's family or firm is, in fact, the secret of success in combatting kidnap and ransom. In the United States, the FBI has always recognized this, and has made it clear that the safe release of the victim has priority over detection and arrest of the kidnappers. As a result, they do get the cooperation and evidence they need, so that, in the 647 reported kidnap cases in the United States between 1934 and 1974, arrests were made in 90 percent of the cases.[4] There can be few crimes, anywhere in the world, in which such a high detection rate has been achieved. Ironically, in countries where the police give priority to detection and arrest, and where they attempt to restrict the payment of ransoms or to ban insurance, both the survival rate of hostages and the arrest rate of kidnappers are far lower.

## Risk Management

The management of a kidnap risk is similar to the management of any other risk: to identify and assess the risk and then to decide how far it is practicable to avoid, reduce, or transfer it, or whether one should just ignore it.

Once again, every security director is familiar with this process in making a fire plan for his premises. He assesses the risk of fire at various points and the cost of the damage it could do. Since this damage is obviously too costly to ignore, he introduces a plan to prevent it, to fight it, and, in case both of these fail, to insure against it.

The approach to the kidnap risk should be similar. The responsible executive assesses the risk and the possible cost of a kidnap in both human and financial terms; he examines the various measures to reduce the risk and the cost of each, in terms not only of direct expenditure but also of inconvenience, loss of efficiency, and hence loss of earnings; he decides how much it is worth paying to reduce the risk and to indemnify against it by insurance; he then makes contingency plans in case it occurs, including the establishment of a shadow crisis management team.

The kidnap risk will obviously vary with the situation in the country concerned: the pattern of crime and political extremism, of previous kidnaps, of the fate of hostages, and of the size of ransoms demanded and paid; also the efficiency and integrity of the security forces and intelligence services, and the effectiveness of the law and its enforcement.

The threat to a corporation will depend upon its location, its prestige, and its reputed wealth; also on its labor relations and the training and security consciousness of its staff.

The threat to each person, whether as a member of the corporation or as a private individual, will depend upon his own reputed wealth and on the publicity impact which his seizure would make; also on how easy he would be to abduct; on how far he necessarily or avoidably follows a publicly known or predictable routine; on the security of his place of work, his residence, and his journeys between them; and on his own attitude to security. Chief executives, chauffeurs, secretaries, or gatekeepers may all be at risk in their different ways, and similar considerations may have to be applied to their families.

In assessing the form in which the threat might materialize, it is necessary to look through the eyes of the local criminal gangs and political extremist groups. The criminals will be primarily seeking maximum profit at minimum risk and are therefore unlikely to kill their victim, no matter how aggressively they threaten to do so unless, in the final stages, they become alarmed that he might later identify them. The aims of political groups will be more diffuse. Their long-term aims may be nationalist, secessionist, religious, or revolutionary; their short-term aims may be ransom money for their party funds, political blackmail (e.g., release of prisoners), publicity, discrediting the government, or, sometimes, the expression of hatred or revenge—or a combination of several of these.

Having taken a cold look at their aims, one must give thought to what kind of actions would best advance these aims. What is the most likely way to get money or gain publicity? Or to apply pressure on the government, or to humiliate it, or to arouse discord and strife?

Next, if a kidnap is considered a likely tactic to achieve these purposes, it is necessary to assess how it might be organized. For an easy target, such as a child walking to school or an executive who drives home in his own car and gets out to open his garage door, a couple of criminals can do the whole job—abduction, incarceration, and negotiation and collection of a ransom. For a man who takes better precautions, enters or leaves his car only when inside a secure perimeter, travels with doors locked, varies his time and route and reports his departures and expected times of arrival, a fairly full surveillance will be done before he is selected and several groups or cells may be involved in his abduction and guarding. For a public figure who moves only with an escort, it is not uncommon for sixty people in a dozen groups to be involved in surveillance, planning, abduction, diversions, getaway, incarceration, and negotiation, collection, and recycling of the ransom money.[5]

All this must be taken into account in making a plan for protection. Since 90 percent of kidnaps take place from a car between home and work, the most fundamental decision is whether to attempt a high standard of protection or to rely instead on a low profile. An armored limousine may cost $200,000. Bodyguards, to be of any use, have to be highly trained and motivated. Since the actual abduction is usually done by a team of at least five, in two cars, a bodyguard is worse than useless unless the men have the skill, morale, and strength to match the attack,[6] and this may require at least one escort car. If this is done, however, the target is likely to become conspicuous and it may be wiser to go right to the other end of the spectrum: for the potential target to travel in a nondescript car from the company car pool, using a different one each day, sitting in front with the driver (if he has one), both of them wearing informal clothing (e.g., open shirts, sweaters, or parkas). In either case, he should vary his time and his route, notify by telephone his expected time of arrival, arrange for gates to be opened by someone from inside or by remote control, and he or his driver or both should be trained in evasive or offensive driving in case of a holdup. He should also have a knowledge of safe places to which to drive in an emergency (e.g., police stations or army barracks) and, if possible, have a two-way car radio. If he does, it is important that the antennas should be concealed, since criminals are used to spotting transmission antennas when looking out for police cars. Alternatively, in some countries having one's car simply disguised as a taxi may overcome this.

Above all, the best protection is *awareness* and a positive attitude toward security. This need cost little or nothing and can be far more effective than expensive equipment or guards, since no serious kidnap attempt by either criminals or political extremists is likely without a thorough surveillance of the movements and lifestyle of the potential victim. This is commonly carried out by people who are (or look like) students, usually a boy and a girl. They will probably have no criminal connections and they will be able to hang around or skip in and out of traffic on a motorcycle without arousing suspicion.[7] They will normally he hired for that one task only, which may last for several weeks or months, and will be paid off when they have made their report. They will be asked particularly to report how easy it will be to abduct the victim with minimum risk of witnesses or pursuit and to suggest a place and a means of doing so. If their surveillance reveals a positive attitude toward security, their leader is more likely to direct them to turn away and seek a softer target elsewhere.

It is this pattern of movement and lifestyle that the experienced anti-kidnap surveyor will examine; his advice will draw attention to vulnerable areas and suggest changes in the pattern in order for one to become a less attractive target.

## Contingency Planning and Crisis Management

Most businesses of substance will have a security director who will be responsible for protection against fire and theft as well as against armed robbery, incendiarism, bombing, and personal attack. He may call in fire surveyors or experts on other kinds of security but he will be responsible for assessing the value of their advice and for any subsequent action upon it. In many fields, requirements will overlap; control of entry and identification of staff and visitors, for example, will be as important for the prevention of theft as for the protection against bombing and personal attack.

If a consultant on kidnap risks is called in, he will first examine these general precautions through the eyes of a potential kidnapper and draw attention to weak points. He will also survey the patterns of life and movements of executives and their families and others most vulnerable to kidnap—again through the eyes of the criminal or political terrorist, or through the eyes of the people they may engage to do their surveillance. He will also advise on contingency planning and crisis management.

In contingency planning for a kidnap crisis, it must be recognized that many agencies and individuals will be involved, both in preparing for the crisis and in handling it if it occurs, and that their interests will often conflict.

First, there are the potential victims, and these will include the chief executives. Except in notoriously high-risk countries such as El Salvador, a chief executive will frequently blench at the thought of disrupting his work and private life and will hunt for arguments not to do so—"It won't happen to me" or "If they want me they'll get me" or "How can I do a decent job if I'm hemmed in by security?" or "I'd rather take the risk than sacrifice all the pleasures of living" or—most insidiously—"It's only my own life I'm risking, anyway." He must be persuaded that this is a grossly selfish attitude. It is *not* only his risk. If he is kidnapped, the effects on his corporation and his family, both financially and in human agony, are likely to be catastrophic.

Then there is the potential victim's family. They must also avoid being targets, and may indeed be more attractive targets than he is. A strong man who will readily lay his own life on the line may give way to a threat to the life of his eight-year-old daughter. If he himself is kidnapped, special care must be taken to prevent a supplementary kidnap of a member of his family, since this will strengthen the kidnapper's hand. The personality of his wife will also affect negotiations for his release. At least one Latin American terrorist group advised its members to select a victim with a strong-willed wife—one who would bang the table to force his firm to pay to secure his release.

There will also be lawyers involved. In some cases the interests of the firm's lawyers and of family lawyers will conflict. A common front should be established in the contingency planning *before* a crisis occurs. Moreover, one of these lawyers—probably one retained by the firm— may be the best man for selection and training as negotiator. Since kidnappers will seldom risk saying in advance when they will next telephone, one or even two relief negotiators may be needed.[8]

A potential victim, especially one under threat in a dangerous country, may well employ his own security advisers and guards for his home and his family, especially if he himself travels a great deal, or if he does not wholly trust the local security companies and guards whom his firm will have to employ. The firm's security officer must certainly be made aware of this so that he can at least coordinate their precautions and ensure that they act in concert in the crisis immediately following a kidnap.

The executives of the victim's firm, each with his own responsibilities (financial, security, public relations, legal, etc.) may well have conflicting attitudes to the problem. If it is a subsidiary, the Corporate

Headquarters of the parent company will also be involved, because any ransom paid must be at the expense of their assets, and they also have to face the problem of staff recruitment and morale. The government in the home country of the parent corporation will also be involved, politically, economically, and diplomatically.

The contingency planner must next consider the government of the country in which the firm is operating, whether his own or a host country. There will again be conflicting interests between, for example, national, provincial, and local administrations; government and opposition; the legislature and its committees; minority, functional, and pressure groups; and, of course, the judiciary. In some countries this is, in fact if not in theory, under the direction of the government. In others, such as Italy, there is a structure of examining magistrates, one of whom is likely to be given overall responsibility for the handling of the case, including direction of the police, from the moment a kidnap is reported.

The police, too, may be fragmented. Italy has three police forces, each under a different ministry: the *carabinieri,* the normal city police, and the fiscal police (who would be closely involved in currency problems arising from payment of a ransom). Some countries follow the American pattern of having large numbers of independent forces responsible to local governments (there are 48 in Greater Los Angeles alone); others have a single police force which may have an involvement with certain political leaders, or be at odds with the army. The police in some countries are notoriously corrupt—a common symptom of this is the coincidence of low police pay and high police recruiting. The security planner working in a strange land must be ready to take great trouble (initially, perhaps, through his Embassy) to make contact with an uncorrupted senior police officer whom he can trust to keep their joint planning on a need-to-know basis.

Then there is the army. Every country has one, and its degree of political control and of cooperation with the police will vary. Some are political, others not; some are corrupt, others not; some are efficient, others not. There will also be intelligence services, sometimes integrated but more often not; the rival intelligence organizations may often be spying primarily on each other. The security planner must know his way around, and find out whom he can trust.

Finally there are the mass media, which can be either a liability or, if their cooperation is obtained, a powerful asset. In most countries, sadly, the media are under direct government control. In others, they may be totally irresponsible, aiming only to compete for readers and listeners at no matter what risk to human life. It is again essential for the security planner (or his public relations colleague) to know his way around, to know how best to keep unscrupulous or hostile journalists away, and, if possible, to develop friendly contacts with some reliable ones, who can be repaid for their cooperation and forbearance by being the first to get news and exclusive comment. None of this, however, will be achieved unless painstaking preparatory work and development of contacts have been done *before* there is a crisis. There must be a predetermined policy, promulgated to all staff likely to be involved, for handling the media in the event of someone being kidnapped. Otherwise, the first hours of a crisis can be damaging, both for the victim and his family or firm.

Among the provisions of a contingency plan should be a personal confidential file for each potential victim, containing such details as his address and telephone number, description of official and family cars, children's schools and regular activities (e.g., ballet class on Tuesdays), the numbers of passports, credit cards, etc., medical data (e.g., blood group, special drugs), up-to-date photographs, and details of family doctor, lawyer, and trusted neighbors and friends. In a high-risk area, it may be desirable to keep samples of handwriting and voice recordings.

Above all, the contingency plan must include the formation of a shadow crisis management team (CMT). It must include the executives responsible for finance, risk management, legal matters, personnel and public relations, and whoever is earmarked to be chief negotiator.

The CMT must plan jointly with selected police officers to a degree which will vary with their reliability. The crisis management plan should include a list of names of police officers who may be informed. It may also be wise to restrict the knowledge of this list to certain named executives or trusted staff. Others in the firm should be instructed to inform one of these staff members—*not* the police directly. In some countries a direct link with the police may be necessary, possibly by radio to overcome cut telephone wires. The police should also be invited to provide the firm with a check list of items on which they will want information.

A proforma should then be prepared to help members of the staff who might receive the first kidnap telephone call ("We've got your boss. Unless you do what we say by . . ."). Playing for time, asking the right questions, and noting details of the voice, background noise, etc., may enormously increase the prospects for the release of the victim and the arrest of the kidnappers. Many firms already have such a proforma by every relevant telephone to deal with bomb calls. An adaption of this proforma will serve for a kidnap call. Again, the first response and the first minutes or hours may be crucial.

The CMT must also develop policies for negotiation and for the payment of ransoms. Blundering into these without prior thought can be disastrous. The team must also organize staff training and orientation, to maintain awareness and security consciousness. Finally, they must constantly review and update the plan to allow for staff postings, a changing threat, and availability of new and better security equipment and techniques.

Once a kidnap has occurred the CMT goes into action. There are two radically different types of situation. One is where the location of the hideout is unknown and the negotiator must rely on the kidnappers contacting him, usually by means of a number of short and brutal telephone calls, with often long and unpredictable intervals in between. The other type is a siege situation, where the location is known, either from the start or because it has been traced, and is besieged by the police. In the first type the negotiation must be done by representatives of the victim's family or firm (wherever the kidnappers choose to telephone). In the second—the siege—it will be done by the police. The first is by far the more difficult of the two. It would clearly be counter-productive to describe the arts of negotiation in a publicly printed journal but, like most arts, they come mainly from practice and experience. Since it is rare for the same firm or family to be picked twice for a kidnap (because once bitten their security will become much better), the lawyer or family member assigned to negotiate will very rarely have done it before. They will therefore be particularly in need of experienced advice. In their first fifty cases Control Risks advised negotiators facing total demands amounting to over $300 million. About $60 million in all was paid in ransoms and all but three of the victims live to tell the tale.

## Notes

1. Anthony A. Cassidy, "Lloyd's Kidnap/Ransom Insurance," *Risk Management*, September 1976.

2. Rupert Cornwell, ''Kidnapping—the peculiarly Italian Crime,'' *Financial Times,* November 14, 1979.

3. The choice of a negotiator is discussed more fully in Richard Clutterbuck, *Kidnap and Ransom: the Response* (Faber and Faber, London and Boston, 1978), pp. 115–17.

4. Brian Jenkins, *Should Corporations be Prevented from Paying Ransoms?* (Rand Corporation, Santa Monica, 1974).

5. The number involved in the kidnapping of Aldo Moro in Rome in 1977 was believed to be over 60. It was probably also of this order in the case of Hanns-Martin Schleyer in Germany in 1977 and of Geoffrey Jackson, the British Ambassador in Uruguay, in 1971. A fuller discussion of the organization of a kidnap may be found in Richard Clutterbuck, op. cit., pp. 57–67.

6. The security industry contains many highly reputable firms but also attracts a number of sharks. Even in sophisticated countries such as the United States and Britain, attempts to enforce high standards of professionalism and integrity—either by voluntary institutions in the industry or by legislation—still have a long way to go. In some countries the hiring of bodyguards is fraught with dangers, ranging from extortion by ''protection racket'' to sheer incompetence. As in many other fields, you get no more than you pay for, but you may get a great deal less. It is wise to check the firm, with an independent source, such as the police (if reliable) or, in the case of a subsidiary, one's own country's embassy.

7. Sir Geoffrey Jackson has given a vivid description of how he detected the surveillance before he was kidnapped in his book *People's Prison* (Faber and Faber, London, 1972), also published as *Surviving the Long Night* (Vanguard, New York, 1974). There is a summary of this in Clutterbuck, op. cit., pp. 58–60.

8. There is a good account of a kidnap negotiation in Italy in the *New York Times Magazine,* November 20, 1977, cited in Clutterbuck, op. cit., pp. 161–64.

# The United Nations Convention Against the Taking of Hostages: Realistic or Rhetoric?

Clive C. Aston

University of London

*Abstract*     In an effort to circumvent the lack of international agreement on needed measures against political terrorism and impelled by the siege of their embassy in Stockholm in 1975, the West German government decided to propose a convention banning a more specific manifestation of terrorism: the taking of hostages. The author reviews the central political issues that have pervaded the debates on this item within the United Nations until its final adoption in 1979. The most crucial issue was whether the scope of the proposed convention should include actions undertaken by those movements engaged in a recognized struggle for national liberation. The resulting compromise required to ensure its adoption by the General Assembly has left the Convention with an inherent tautology which will undoubtedly hinder and may prevent its general ratification and subsequent entry into force.

The precipitating motivation behind many instruments of international legislation against terrorism can often be linked to a single, specific incident. For example, the League of Nations Convention for the Prevention and Punishment of Terrorism was stimulated by the assassination of King Alexander of Yugoslavia and Louis Barthou, the French Foreign Minister, by a member of the Ustachi on October 9, 1934. Similarly, the Dutch government's proposal that led to the 1973 Convention on the Prevention and Punishment of Crimes Against Internationally Protected Persons, Including Diplomatic Agents, arose as a response to the Amboinese siege of the Indonesian ambassador's residence in The Hague on April 31, 1970. In the case of the United Nations debates on a draft convention against the taking of hostages, the impetus can be traced to a shocked moral reaction by the government of the Federal Republic of Germany to the siege of its embassy in Stockholm on April 24, 1975 by members of the Holger Meins Kommando.

In order to circumvent a repetition of the problems that resulted in the suspension of the Ad Hoc Committee on International Terrorism after its first session in 1973, the initial draft convention submitted by West Germany attempted to depoliticize the act of taking hostages, as it had already successfully done in regard to the Council of Europe Convention on the Suppression of Terrorism.[1] However, it soon became apparent that whereas a regional convention of this type could be arrived at by countries sharing fairly common basic values and norms, this was simply not feasible within the international community. It seems, moreover, and to paraphrase slightly, that "one man's hostage-taker is another man's freedom fighter." Consequently, the finalized Convention Against the Taking of Hostages now open for signature is not only markedly different in tone and substance but, more remarkably, contains an inherent tautology primarily insisted upon by the so-called Third World countries. To understand how this has occurred, it is necessary to review the four years of debates on this item within the United Nations.

In January 1976, the West German government began informal discussions with other states on a worldwide basis aimed at securing support for a United Nations initiative against the taking of hostages by terrorists. Encouraged by the positive approach adopted by many states and especially by the unanimous endorsement of a draft convention on terrorism by the Ministers of Justice of the Council of Europe on June 5, Hans-Dietrich Genscher, the West German Vice-Chancellor and Foreign Minister, delivered a letter to the Secretary-General of the United Nations on September 28 requesting the inclusion on the agenda of the 31st Session of "an important and urgent matter, of a separate item entitled 'Drafting of an international convention against the taking of hostages.' "[2] Throughout the letter and explanatory memorandum, Genscher scrupulously avoided the use of the term "terrorism" because, as he candidly admitted, "we wanted to take an initiative which has a chance of success in the United Nations."[3] Rather, he stressed ''that the taking of innocent hostages for whatever purposes constitutes an act which is absolutely intolerable and incompatible with universally accepted standards of human conduct.''[4] He also pointed out that the international community owed it to its own self-respect to take effective action against an act which was already prohibited in time of war and on board civilian aircraft.

At its 16th plenary meeting on October 4, the General Assembly, acting on the recommendation of the General Committee,[5] allocated the item to the Sixth (Legal) Committee.[6] The Sixth Committee decided to discuss the item at four meetings on November 22–23.[7] At its 55th meeting, four days later than planned, it began its deliberations when the representative from West Germany introduced a draft resolution on behalf of his own and sixteen other states.[8] The draft resolution was humanitarian in tone and still avoided any connection between hostage-taking and the thornier issue of terrorism.[9] Essentially, it was a procedural resolution and merely called for the establishment of an Ad Hoc Committee charged with a mandate to draw up an international convention ''on the basis that the taking of hostages should be condemned, prohibited and punished and that persons who perpetrate such acts should be prosecuted or extradited for the purpose of prosecution.''[10] The West German representative explained that

> . . . the draft resolution was to establish the prerequisites for a rational discussion of the measures which might be adopted against the taking of hostages. . . . The sponsors believed a particularly appropriate forum for this discussion would be an ad hoc committee. Such a committee was also the proper place to dissipate doubts about political consequences of such a convention and to consider aspects of criminal law, law of extradition and the law of asylum, and other issues which would also be involved.[11]

One such issue that was immediately and portentously raised was brought up by the representative of Portugal and concerned the particular innocence of hostages who were ''innocent because they were entirely unconnected with the situation which had provoked the act of their captors.''[12]

It did not take long, however, for the general debate to move from procedural to more substantive issues along predictable bloc lines. At the 56th meeting of the Sixth Committee, the representative from Upper

Volta stressed that the real issue under discussion was one of justifying terrorism which "no matter how repugnant it appeared, had a motivation that all lovers of justice, freedom and human dignity could understand, even if they disapproved of it."[13] In what was to become one of the main recurring themes from then on, the representative from Romania brought the same issue into sharper focus by stating that his government "rejected any attempt to compare the struggle of peoples for national liberation with international terrorism."[14] At the next meeting, the Algerian representative, in keeping with the dictates of his country's constitution, outlined the position of the African group by arguing:

> In examining the item under consideration, the Committee should not, like a public prosecutor seeking retribution, set up the legal structure for an international manhunt in disregard of such well-established concepts of international law as the basic distinction between political offences and offences under the general law and the law of asylum. Instead, it should endeavour to understand those who were in despair and who, because of the international community's failure to act, were the real outcasts in an unjust world. . . .[15]
>
> Unless the problem was tackled at the root, any new convention might well be ineffectual, for no international law could match the despair of those who, before seeking to endanger the lives of others, had already sacrificed their own lives for the ideas to which they wished to draw the world's attention. That, in fact, was often the ransom they were seeking.[16]

This position was tentatively proposed as an additional preambular paragraph, to follow the seventh preambular paragraph of the West German resolution, at the 58th meeting by the representative from Somalia but not formally introduced as an amendment.[17]

The only two amendments that were formally introduced at this early stage also arose at the 58th meeting. These were submitted by the Libyan representative who sought to incorporate the term "innocent" used in the explanatory memorandum of Genscher's letter and by several other representatives during the debate, a point overlooked by the press at the time.[18] Specifically:

> (a) Insert the word 'innocent' before the word 'hostage' in the fourth, seventh and eighth paragraphs of the preamble and in operative paragraphs 1, 5 and 7;

(b) Replace operative paragraph 3 with the following: '3. *Requests* the Committee to draft at the earliest possible date an international convention against the taking of innocent hostages.'[19]

Other, generally pro-Western representatives contested this amendment because of its tautological nature and argued that its adoption would create a dangerous precedent. For example, the representative from Uruguay stated:

It would be necessary to specify very clearly who was to decide whether hostages were innocent or not, failing which tacit authority might be conferred on the perpetrators of the crime to be the first to make such a decision. The possibility that some person would subsequently endorse that decision would encourage the taking of hostages and, as a result, insecurity, far from being dispelled, would persist.[20]

At the next meeting, the 69th, when the draft resolution was again discussed, the Libyan representative indicated he would withdraw his amendment but would continue to press the issue in the ad hoc committee. In return, the West German representative announced that a compromise draft resolution had been negotiated by a group of five countries from the non-aligned bloc and formally introduced it on behalf of his own and thirty-five other states.[21] The primary revision that had been negotiated concerned operative paragraph 3 and its requirement of basing the enforcement procedures of the proposed convention on the priciple of *aut dedere aut punire* (to extradite or to prosecute). This had been removed to overcome the objection that operative paragraph 3 raised a substantive issue and thereby prejudged the work of the ad hoc committee. The representative from Somalia had earlier pointed out, in an obvious reference to the rescue mission undertaken at Entebbe by Israeli commandos:

The provisions of paragraph 3 as it stood could have serious repercussions for States which, for humanitarian reasons, provided refuge to hijackers and hostages. Such States could be exposed to a situation in which their sovereignty and territorial integrity could be illegally violated by the unilateral action of another State claiming national allegiance to the hostages. Experience had shown that States receiving hostages could suffer blatant aggression by other interested parties.[22]

Accordingly, the revised operative paragraph 3 now only referred to authorizing the committee "to consider suggestions and proposals from any State" on enforcement procedures.

The following day, December 10, the Sixth Committee adopted the revised draft resolution by consensus and recommended that the General Assembly follow suit. At its 99th plenary meeting on December 15, the General Assembly did so and thereby established an Ad Hoc Committee on the Drafting of an International Convention Against the Taking of Hostages. The Committee was to be composed of thirty-five Member States who were to be appointed by the President of the General Assembly "on the basis of equitable geographical distribution and of representation of the principal legal systems of the world."[23]

On June 28, 1977, the President of the General Assembly informed the Secretary-General that he had appointed thirty-four of the thirty-five members.[24] One such member was the United Kingdom who, on December 15, 1976, had voted against the extension of the mandate of the Ad Hoc Committee on International Terrorism.[25]

The Ad Hoc Committee first met as a body on August 1, 1977 at the United Nations Headquarters in New York. At its second meeting, the election of officers had to be postponed until the following day as the African group had not yet decided upon a candidate for Chairman. At the third meeting, a consensus had been achieved by the regional groups and Mr. Leslie O. Harriman (Nigeria) was elected Chairman by acclamation as were the Vice-Chairmen from Iran, West Germany, and Nicaragua. Also at the 3rd meeting, West Germany submitted a working paper containing a draft convention.[26] However, at the suggestion of the representative from the United Republic of Tanzania, it was decided to delay any discussion of concrete proposals, as required by the General Assembly resolution in operative paragraph 3, in favor of a general debate until the 10th meeting.

Throughout the debate of the next six meetings, various and again predictable themes were put forward by the representatives from the regional groups. Those from the pro-Western group[26A] argued in favor of a convention, such as the West German one, which would espouse Western humanitarian values and norms of behavior. The convention would have to be based on the principle of "extradite or prosecute" with no allowances being made for the political motivation of the hostage-takers; otherwise it "would amount to legitimizing a crime which was repugnant to the conscience of mankind or would maintain a climate of tension between the States concerned . . . which an organization whose main purpose was the maintenance of peace between peoples should avoid at any cost.''[27] It was also argued that a convention of this type would be the surest method of combatting hostage-taking as ''the only effective means of reducing, if not eliminating, that kind of criminal activity was to ensure that the perpetrators fully understood from the outset that they could not escape without severe punishment.''[28]

On the other hand, the African and Soviet bloc groups[29] felt the West German initiative was too hasty and ''related to only one aspect of violence and might well delay consideration of an overall solution to a problem which affected the sacred rights of human beings, their lives and freedom.''[30] Indeed, it was held:

> . . . that the taking of hostages was only one aspect of the broader problem of international terrorism, and it was therefore clear that, if the problem was to be approached in the proper manner and in all its aspects, including the preparation of a draft convention, account must not fail to be taken of relevant objective factors connected with international terrorism and of the causes of that phenomenon. Otherwise, the measures adopted would prove illusory.[31]

Moreover, the convention:

> . . . should recognize the legitimacy of the struggle of national liberation movements and the inalienable right of freedom fighters to take up arms to fight their oppressors. The oppressed peoples and colonial peoples who were held in perpetual bondage could not be stopped from taking oppressors hostage, if that became inevitable.[32]

The 9th meeting was suspended early at the suggestion of the Algerian representative because the ''African group would like to consider the organization of future work.''[33] It was also decided to have the Secretariat draw up an analytical summary of the general debate listing the various proposals that had been put forward.

The work on drawing up a draft convention began during the 10th meeting when the West German representative explained the working paper his delegation had earlier submitted. The explanation was greeted with gratification by the Algerian representative because the committee could now "verify that the document really belonged to the Federal Republic of Germany and not to the United Kingdom or the United States of America."[34]

What followed was to change the complexion of the debates for the next three years and drastically alter not only the structure of the proposed convention but virtually contradict and nullify an earlier gain the African group had made. It must be remembered that only two months prior to this meeting, the African group had succeeded in getting the General Assembly to adopt two Additional Protocols to the Geneva Conventions of 1949 that effectively internationalized internal struggles by national liberation movements. Once ratified, these Protocols will afford liberation movements the same status previously accorded only to the recognized armed forces of the combatant states. In keeping with the earlier Geneva Conventions, both Protocols specifically prohibit the taking of hostages "at any time and in any place whatsoever, whether committed by civilian or by military agents."[35]

At the 10th meeting, the representative from the United Republic of Tanzania submitted a proposed amendment that constituted the African group's conception of the scope of the draft convention:

> For the purposes of this Convention, the term 'taking of hostages' shall not include any act or acts carried out in the process of national liberation against colonial rule, racist or foreign regimes, by liberation movements recognized by the United Nations or regional organizations.[36]

At the following meeting, the American representative predictably argued against the Tanzanian proposal on the grounds that "just as certain forms of violence, such as acts committed against protected persons, including diplomatic agents, were inadmissible regardless of the circumstances, so the act of taking hostages which endangered human lives was inadmissible in all cases."[37] This notion was reverted to at the 12th meeting by the representative from the United Kingdom who stated that the Tanzanian proposal was astonishing because it "did not actually constitute a definition but rather established an exception, namely, that certain acts involving the taking of hostages were not to be considered as such and that while they were impermissible they were not a matter which fell within the scope of the convention."[38]

At the 14th meeting, the West German representative assured the African group that the draft convention was not aimed at infringing upon any of the rights of national liberation movements but that it was solely intended to fill the gaps in existing international legislation against the taking of hostages. Moreover, should the Tanzanian proposal be adopted, he was afraid that ''the convention would be interpreted as relieving liberation movements of their obligations under international law and would prove a setback to the efforts to humanize conflict.''[39]

The Tanzanian representative stated that if his delegation's provision was misinterpreted as an open license for liberation movements to take hostages, he ''would not be surprised, since liberation movements have in the past been labelled as terroristic and their actions would continue to be misinterpreted whether or not the provision was included in the convention.''[40] Nonetheless, he declared that the African group would insist upon the general idea of his provision being incorporated into any future convention as a bare minimum.

A new twist to the growing controversy over the definition of hostage-taking was added during the 14th meeting by the Libyan representative. He proposed that:

For the purposes of this Convention, the term 'taking of hostages' is the seizure or detention, not only of a person or persons, but also of masses under colonial, racist or foreign domination, in a way that threatens him or them with death, or severe injury or deprives him or them of their fundamental freedoms.[41]

The representative from Italy immediately countered by arguing that ''the definition of 'taking of hostages' provided in the draft convention was entirely satisfactory.''[42]

Unsurprisingly, the discussions began to degenerate to the stage where the Algerian representative remarked ''that the Committee's discussions lacked cohesion.''[43] The representative from the United Kingdom was more optimistic because it ''had become clear that there were opposing views on the question of national liberation movements, and it might take some time to find a solution, but at least the problem had been clearly defined.''[44]

The 15th meeting opened with no signs of improvement in the dialogue between the two groups. The representative from Democratic Yemen accurately identified the dilemma by stating:

. . . that no real progress had been made in the work of the Committee because members had avoided confronting the real issue, which was neither juridical nor a matter of drafting. The issue was political in nature. One of the two prevailing views was that the draft convention should be all-inclusive and applicable to national liberation movements, while the other was that the convention should not apply to acts carried out by national liberation movements in the course of their struggle against colonialism, racism, *apartheid* and foreign domination. . . . The problem was not a disagreement between two delegations but rather a difference of political philosophies.[45]

In an effort to overcome this, the Chairman suggested that issues of substance, "including the scope of the convention, the relationship of the convention to other legal instruments, and the position of the liberation movements,"[46] be discussed in private consultations among members.

A spirit of compromise appears to have prevailed between the groups as the 16th meeting opened and once more began to discuss substantive issues. Now, however, the disagreements had become intra-group in nature. The Dutch representative questioned the efficacy of paragraph 1 (b) of the West German draft[47] and the American representative disagreed with the substance of paragraph 7.[48] Once again, the meeting was suspended to allow delegates to search for alternatives during informal discussions.

West Germany opened the 17th meeting by continuing this intra-group dispute and disagreed with the need for the amendments proposed by Canada, Chile, France, and the Netherlands. The representative from Mexico finally suggested that a compromise solution might still be found to overcome the impasse on the question of hostage-taking by liberation movements, a view promptly endorsed by Canada and the Philippines.

The agenda called for the adoption of the Committee's report by the 18th meeting but, as the Rapporteur pointed out, "the various suggestions that had been made as to the content and structure of the final report were mutually exclusive, and he needed some guidance from the Committee in order to choose between them."[49] Here then was an issue behind which the various groups could again close ranks. The representative from Guinea argued "that the draft report reflected accurately the work of the current session"[50] whereas the American representative stated that "his delegation was in no position to agree to the draft report since it represented only a small part of the full report of the Ad Hoc Committee."[51] Three concrete suggestions were subsequently put forward and reiterated by the Chairman as, "the report should include a summary of the general debate, a summary of the entire debate, or all the summary records and the various working papers."[52] In the end, the representative from Guinea suggested as a compromise that the Rapporteur write a short summary of the discussions and include all relevant documents as an annex.

At its final meeting of 1977, on August 19, the Committee adopted the report[53] though not without reservations being voiced by some representatives. The Mexican representative, for example, did not object "because it could hardly object to something that did not say anything."[54] The American representative was similarly disappointed that "the Committee could merely state that it had had a useful session, without being able to say either how or why it had been useful."[55]

The Committee also adopted a draft resolution by consensus which recommended that the General Assembly should invite it to continue its work in 1978.[56]

The Sixth Committee began considering the report at its 59th meeting on November 30. While the majority of delegates argued in favor of extending the mandate, representatives from the Soviet bloc "wondered whether it would not be preferable to entrust the drafting of a convention on the taking of hostages to the Ad Hoc Committee on International Terrorism."[57] Nonetheless, at its 69th meeting, on December 12, the Sixth Committee adopted a decision by consensus recommending the Ad Hoc Committee's mandate be extended.[58] The General Assembly considered the recommendation at its 105th plenary meeting on December 16 and adopted resolution 32/148 thereby extending the mandate.

The Ad Hoc Committee resumed its work as a body on February 6, 1978 at the United Nations Headquarters in Geneva and promptly reelected its officers. The 20th meeting was then suspended to again allow for informal discussions to take place on the organization of work they would subsequently follow.

A more pragmatic approach was begun at the 21st meeting with a second reading of the West German draft convention. During the next four meetings, Articles 2-11 were discussed and amendments suggested. The difficulties encountered earlier began again when, at the 24th meeting, the Committee turned to Article 1. The Algerian representative, supported by the representative from the USSR, proposed that the Committee first turn its attention to the draft preamble submitted by his delegation[59] before discussing further draft articles. To prevent a repeat of the earlier outbursts, the meeting was suspended again to allow for informal discussions to take place on the procedure to be followed.

Prior to the next meeting, a compromise procedure had been arrived at and was presented by the Chairman at the opening of the 25th meeting:

> At the close of the meeting, the officers had decided to suggest to the plenary Committee the establishment of two working groups open to all interested delegations in which no summary records would be taken of the proceedings. Working Group I would examine the thornier questions connected with the drafting of an international convention against the taking of hostages, and would try to find some common ground by means of consultations. Working Group II would concern itself with draft articles that were non-controversial or on which Working Group I had come to an agreement; it would in fact be the drafting group.[60]

The Committee agreed to this and, six days later, again met in plenary to hear the progress reports of the two Working Groups. The Chairman of Working Group I, who was also the Chairman of the Ad Hoc Committee, concluded his report by stating:

> . . . the questions of the right of asylum and respect for the sovereignty and territorial integrity of States with regard to the release of hostages constituted minor problems which could be settled by rewording the relevant provisions of the proposed convention in the light of the suggestions made during the negotiations. In spite of the efforts already made, the most difficult question—safeguarding the rights of national liberation movements—required further negotiations for a generally agreed solution to be reached.[61]

The Chairman of Working Group II stated that ''the Group had almost reached agreement on a text acceptable to the majority of the members of the Committee.''[62] However, Article 5, concerning jurisdiction, continued to pose problems and further negotiations were required to find a compromise. The Committee agreed to continue to meet in working groups and would meet again in plenary in five days' time.

At the 27th meeting, the French representative introduced an additional preambular paragraph stating that "the taking of hostages is and must be proscribed always, everywhere and in all circumstances.'"[63] A second amendment he introduced concerned the need to specify the scope of the convention "which could be summed up in the following way: the convention must only punish acts of hostage-taking, but it must punish them all.'"[64] Predictably, this was not well received by the African group who were arguing for a complete ban on rescue missions such as the Entebbe one and, consequently, discussions had to continue with the immediate result that the reports of the two Working Groups were not yet available.

The 28th meeting opened with the Chairman inviting members to consider the reports of the two Working Groups.[65] The Algerian representative stated that, although the session had been extremely fruitful, divergent and utterly opposing views on the scope of the convention still remained. Moreover:

> Like the delegations of all the non-aligned countries, his own delegation had always been determined to find common ground and to devise a legal instrument which would provide the necessary legal framework for the effective prevention and punishment of hostage-taking without prejudicing the rights of peoples struggling against colonial and racist regimes, *apartheid* and all forms of foreign domination or jeopardizing the already precarious resources available to them for that purpose.[66]

The American representative replied that in his opinion:

> . . . the convention must represent a major step forward in ensuring respect for human life and freedom in all circumstances. Certain cases of hostage-taking could therefore not be excluded from the scope of the convention only because those responsible for them happened to have the support of public opinion. Whatever their motives, acts of hostage-taking were unacceptable.[67]

The focus of this ubiquitous intergroup dispute soon shifted from a substantive to a procedural issue and was particularly evident with regard to paragraph 3 of the report of Working Group I which concerned the scope of the proposed convention. A compromise solution was finally suggested by the Canadian representative and subsequently adopted. This stated:

. . . the negotiations revolved around the generally agreed principle that the taking of hostages was an act prohibited under international law. In this respect, there was general agreement that no one should be granted an open licence for taking hostages.[68]

The 29th meeting on February 24 continued the discussion of the two reports. After the approval of further amendments to the report of Working Group I, the entire report was approved. As Working Group II's report dealt with noncontroversial articles, there were few suggested amendments and the report was quickly adopted. Finally, a decision was reached to annex the two reports to the general report of the Committee to the General Assembly which was subsequently adopted. A draft resolution was also adopted recommending that the General Assembly invite the Committee to continue its work in 1979.[69]

Before the closure of the 1978 session, numerous representatives praised the spirit of compromise that had prevailed during the discussions. However, the representative from the USSR stressed "that the success of their efforts would largely depend on how far they were prepared to take the realities of the present-day into account."[70]

The Sixth Committee began its consideration of the report at their 44th meeting on November 10. One of those who argued in favor of the extension of the Committee's mandate was the observer from the Palestine Liberation Organization, who stated:

The P.L.O. . . . had always adopted an unequivocal attitude with regard to the taking of hostages and had always opposed acts of violence against innocent persons perpetrated by individuals or groups of any kind. . . . The ideal of national liberation movements in their unequal and relentless struggle against the forces of colonialism, racism and occupation, remained the protection of intrinsic human rights and the triumph of freedom and self-determination.[71]

His delegation would continue to work within the Committee in the same constructive way, in order to eradicate the phenomenon of the taking of hostages.[72]

At its 53rd meeting, on November 21, the Sixth Committee adopted a resolution by consensus recommending that the mandate of the Ad Hoc Committee be extended.[73] As all the members of the General Assembly are also members of the Sixth Committee, the extension was assured and accordingly, at its 63rd plenary meeting on November 29, the General Assembly adopted resolution 33/19, thereby inviting the Ad Hoc Committee to continue its work in 1979.[74]

The Committee resumed its work on January 29, 1979 at the United Nations Headquarters in Geneva. Three days earlier, the President of the General Assembly had notified the Secretary-General that Bulgaria had been appointed the thirty-fifth member of the Committee.[75] At its 30th meeting, officers from the same four countries were reelected to the same posts, the two Working Groups were reestablished and the Committee decided to resume its work at the point where it had left off during the previous session.

Working Group I held two meetings and first focused on the question of hostage-taking by national liberation movements. A final compromise solution was accepted as "establishing an equitable balance between the desired objectives."[76] The text that had been decided upon and had caused so much friction during the earlier debates, was incorporated as Article 12 (1) of the draft convention and stated:

In so far as the Geneva Conventions of 1949 for the protection of war victims or the Additional Protocols to those Conventions are applicable to a particular act of hostage-taking, and in so far as States Parties to this Convention are bound under those Conventions to prosecute or hand over the hostage-taker, the present Convention shall not apply to an act of hostage-taking committed in the course of armed conflicts as defined in the Geneva Conventions of 1949 and the Protocols thereto, including armed conflicts mentioned in article 1, paragraph 4, of Additional Protocol I of 1977, in which peoples are fighting against colonial domination and alien occupation and racist regimes in the exercise of their right of self-determination, as enshrined in the Charter of the United Nations and the Declaration on Principles of International Law concerning Friendly Relations and Co-operation among States in Accordance with the Charter of the United Nations.[77]

The second major political question that had to be resolved concerned the respect for the principle of sovereignty and territorial integrity of states under the pretext of rescuing hostages. A compromise solution was also achieved on this issue and accepted as Article 13 of the draft convention:

Nothing in this Convention shall be construed as justifying the violation, in contravention of the Charter of the United Nations, of the territorial integrity or political independence of a State.[78]

The final question dealt with by Working Group I was that of extradition and the right of asylum. Although no compromise was reached, one text received widespread support and was included as Article 14 as a basis for future discussions:

> None of the provisions of this Convention shall be interpreted as impairing the right of asylum. This provision shall not however affect the obligations of Contracting States under the Convention.[79]

The report of Working Group I concluded by stating:

> . . . the constructive and co-operative attitude of all members of the working group was essential for the realization of its objectives. It is to be hoped that the successful achievements indicated above . . . will be responded to with the same positive spirit in other forums.[80]

Working Group II held fourteen meetings between January 30 and February 16 when it carried out a third reading of Articles 1–11 and considered proposals for new articles. General agreement was reached on all the articles, though some were first amended. A preamble was suggested by the representative from the USSR and, although included in the draft, several delegates considered it premature to pronounce themselves on it at that stage:

> *Being convinced* that it is urgently necessary to develop international co-operation between States in devising and adopting effective measures for the prevention, prosecution and punishment of all acts of hostage-taking as manifestations of international terrorism, . . .[81]

Finally, after four years and thirty-five meetings, on February 16, 1979, the Ad Hoc Committee approved the two reports and adopted them as part of its general report to the General Assembly.[82] Far more importantly, they were able to include a finalized draft convention and recommend it to the General Assembly for its consideration and adoption.[83]

The general report and draft convention were considered by the Sixth

(Legal) Committee and adopted without a vote on December 9. On December 17, both were also adopted without amendments by consensus by the General Assembly. The Convention is accordingly now open for signature and will come into force thirty days after the deposit of the twenty-second instrument of ratification.

At the time of writing (March 1980) no country has yet ratified the Convention. Nevertheless, by way of a conclusion, it is apt to speculate what the prospects for general ratification are and what the likely effect the Convention will subsequently have if entered into force.

Initially, the prospects for ratification appear to be quite good if for no other reason than that the Western group has secured the support and agreement of Algeria, Libya and the other traditional supporters of what are loosely termed terrorist groups on the need for an international convention against hostage-taking. That in itself must be seen as a positive achievement. Similarly, the African group has secured Western agreement that the Convention will not be applied to national liberation movements. Consequently, both sides appear to gain from the compromise between a fundamentally moral issue from the former perspective and a fundamentally political issue from the latter. However, it is because of this very compromise that the Convention is unlikely to be generally ratified and, even if it were, it would largely be ineffectual.

The West German intention was to close the gap in existing legislation against the taking of hostages. Here the Convention fails. The only acts which are covered are those which contain an international element, thereby leaving it to the individual state to enact legislation against purely internal acts, such as those conducted by the Italian Brigate Rosse. Even if the act satisfies this criterion, it must then involve demands upon a third party. This, surprisingly, is not always the case and, indeed, of the thirty-three incidents in Western Europe between 1968 and 1978 that can be termed as involving an international element,[84] eleven involved no demands at all.

Similarly, the West German intention was to depoliticize hostage-taking and treat it as a common crime. That would then leave the way clear to base the enforcement procedures of the convention on the principle of "extradite or prosecute." Such a move had earlier been generally successful within the Council of Europe and only Malta and the Republic of Ireland felt unable to sign the resulting convention. From the point of view of the African group, however, this initiative was welcomed as long as it did not impinge upon the rights of national liberation movements to use whatever means at their disposal to conduct their struggle. What the West Germans had to be content with was the fact that most Third World and Soviet bloc countries dichotomize between terrorist groups and groups involved in national liberation, as many of the current Third World regimes once were themselves. While the former are indeed to be condemned, the latter are to be supported. In fact, the provision to aid liberation movements is specifically written into many constitutions, such as Article 13 of the Cuban Constitution. It is hardly surprising, therefore, that the enforcement procedures suggested in the West German proposal proved unacceptable and had to be substantially watered down to the point where Article 14 of the Convention now specifies that the right of asylum shall not be impaired.

The most tautological provision of the entire Convention involves Article 12 (1) whereby hostage-taking by liberation movements is recognized as a legitimate part of their struggle as defined in Article 1 (4) of the Additional Protocol I of June 1977. Incredibly, under the same Protocol, Article 75, s.2 (c) expressly prohibits the taking of hostages by liberation movements at any time and in any place whatsoever. Accordingly, the ratification of the Protocol appears to preclude the ratification of the Convention.

While it was perhaps too much to have expected the United Nations to have been capable of taking effective action against a phenomenon on which opinions and views are so strongly held and so utterly divergent, the Convention remains an unfortunately accurate reflection of the realities of the present world. Nor is legislation against terrorism a panacea. Concerted action aimed at eliminating or at least identifying the underlying sources of structural violence, goal frustration, and socioeconomic inequalities that are often blamed as the precipitants of terrorist behavior will undoubtedly help. Nonetheless, the fact remains that acts of hostage-taking will continue, and probably increase, because it is a proven, effective means of focusing the attention of a largely uncaring world on causes and issues generally overlooked. More despairingly, it has become glamorous.

## Notes

1. *European Treaty Series,* No. 90, especially Article I.
2. U.N. Document A/31/242. Genscher also misleadingly stated that in

"many cases the incident ends with the deliberate killing of the hostages" (Ibid., paragraph 1). Of the fifty-eight hostage incidents (excluding skyjackings) in Western Europe between 1968 and the time of his letter in 1976, only two kidnappings and two sieges ended in the deliberate killing of the hostages by the terrorists.

3. *FBIS,* September 24, 1976, J3.

4. A/31/242, ibid., paragraph 5.

5. A/BUR/31/SR.2.

6. A/C.6/31/3.

7. A/C.6/31/2/Add.1.

8. A/C.6/31/L.10 reprinted as A/31/430, paragraph 4. The other sponsors of the West German draft resolution were: Austria, the Central African Republic, Colombia, Costa Rica, Denmark, Ecuador, Iran, Italy, Liberia, Luxembourg, Nepal, the Netherlands, Surinam, Sweden, Turkey, and Venezuela.

9. Interestingly enough, only two of the original sponsoring states did connect hostage-taking to terrorism during the debates in the Sixth Committee (Colombia and Nepal).

10. A/C.6/31/L.10, paragraph 3.

11. A/C.6/31/SR.54, paragraph 3.

12. Ibid., paragraph 7.

13. A/C.6/31/SR.56, paragraph 2.

14. Ibid., paragraph 10.

15. A/C.6/31/SR.57, paragraph 54.

16. Ibid., paragraph 56.

17. A/C.6/31/SR.58, paragraph 54. This was expressed as: *Recognizing* also the need to give due consideration to the underlying causes of acts involving the taking of hostages; . . .

18. See for example, the *International Herald Tribune,* November 27, 1976, and the *New York Times,* December 10, 1976.

19. A/C.6/31/L.11 reprinted as A/31/430, paragraph 5.

20. A/C.6/31/SR.58 paragraph 14.

21. A/C.6/31/L.10/Rev. 1 reprinted as A/31/430, paragraph 6. The other sponsors of the West German draft resolution were: Austria, Barbados, Belgium, Bolivia, Canada, the Central African Republic, Chile, Colombia, Costa Rica, Denmark, Ecuador, El Salvador, France, Greece, Grenada, Iran, Ireland, Italy, Japan, Liberia, Luxembourg, Nepal, the Netherlands, Nicaragua, Norway, the Philippines, Portugal, Singapore, Surinam, Sweden, Turkey, the United Kingdom, the United States, and Venezuela.

22. A/C.6/31/SR.58 paragraph 55.

23. General Assembly Resolution 31/103, operative paragraph 2.

24. A/31/479 and Add. 1.

25. For the reasons the United Kingdom voted against this resolution, see *Official Records of the General Assembly, Thirty-first Session, Plenary Meetings,* vol. III, p. 1487, paragraph 37.

26. A/AC.188/L. 3 reprinted in Supplement No. 39, A/32/39, pp. 106–10.

26A. Of the twenty-six delegates who spoke during the general debate, the following thirteen argued the same pro-Western line: Canada, Chile, France, the Federal Republic of Germany, Italy, Japan, Nicaragua, the Philippines, Surinam, Sweden, the United Kingdom, the United States of America, and Venezuela.

27. Statement by the Chilean representative during the 4th meeting, A/32/39, p. 18, paragraph 8.

28. Statement by the Italian representative during the 5th meeting, ibid., p. 23, paragraph 18.

29. Of the twenty-six delegates who spoke during the general debate, the following thirteen argued the same pro-African line: Algeria, Egypt, Guinea, Iran, Jordan, Lesotho, the Libyan Arab Jamahiriya, Mexico, Poland, the Syrian Arab Republic, the USSR, the United Republic of Tanzania, and Yugoslavia.

30. Statement by the Algerian representative during the 8th meeting, A/32/39, p. 30, paragraph 2.

31. Statement by the representative from the USSR during the 8th meeting, ibid., p. 31, paragraph 8.

32. Statement by the Tanzanian representative during the 8th meeting, ibid., p. 35, paragraph 28.

33. Statement by the Algerian representative during the 9th meeting, ibid., p. 42, paragraph 29.

34. Statement by the Algerian representative during the 10th meeting, ibid., p. 48, paragraph 13.

35. A/32/144, Article 75, s.2 (c).

36. Statement by the Tanzanian representative during the 10th meeting, A/32/39, p. 49, paragraph 15, submitted as A/AC.188/L.5.

37. Statement by the American representative during the 11th meeting, ibid., p. 55, paragraph 26.

38. Statement by the representative from the United Kingdom during the 12th meeting, ibid., pp. 60–61, paragraph 4.

39. Statement by the West German representative during the 13th meeting, ibid., p. 70, paragraph 10.

40. Statement by the Tanzanian representative during the 13th meeting, ibid., p. 71, paragraph 13.

41. Statement by the Libyan representative during the 14th meeting, ibid., p. 75, paragraph 9, submitted as A/AC.188/L.9.

42. Statement by the Italian representative during the 14th meeting, ibid., p. 78, paragraph 27.

43. Statement by the Algerian representative during the 14th meeting, ibid., p. 81, paragraph 46.

44. Statement by the representative from the United Kingdom during the 14th meeting, ibid., p. 81, paragraph 45.

45. Statement by the representative from Democratic Yemen during the 15th meeting, ibid., p. 83, paragraph 4.

46. Statement by the Chairman during the 15th meeting, ibid., p. 87, paragraph 23.

47. Statement by the representative from the Netherlands during the 16th meeting, ibid., p. 89, paragraph 7.

48. Statement by the American representative during the 16th meeting, ibid., p. 89, paragraph 10.

49. Statement by the Rapporteur during the 18th meeting, ibid., p. 96, paragraph 3.

50. Statement by the representative from Guinea during the 18th meeting, ibid., p. 96, paragraph 7.

51. Statement by the American representative during the 18th meeting, ibid., p. 96, paragraph 6.

52. Statement by the Chairman during the 18th meeting, ibid., p. 95, paragraph 10.

53. A/AC.188/L.15 reprinted in ibid., pp. 1–5.

54. Statement by the Mexican representative during the 19th meeting, ibid., p. 104, paragraph 7.

55. Statement by the American representative during the 19th meeting, ibid., p. 105, paragraph 12.

56. A/AC.188/L.17 reprinted in ibid., p. 5.

57. Statement by the representative from the USSR during the 60th meeting, A/C.6/32/SR.60, paragraph 21.

58. Resolution A/C.6/32/L.10 reprinted in A/C.6/32/SR.69, paragraph 3.

59. A/AC.188/L.4 reprinted in A/32/39, pp. 110–11.

60. Statement by the Chairman during the 25th meeting, A/33/39, p. 56, paragraph 1.

61. Statement by the Chairman during the 26th meeting, ibid., p. 58, paragraph 6.

62. Statement by the West German representative during the 26th meeting, ibid., p. 59, paragraph 9.

63. Statement by the French representative during the 27th meeting, ibid., p. 63, paragraph 2, submitted as A/AC.188/L.20.

64. Ibid., paragraph 3.

65. A/AC.188/L.22 and A/AC.188/L.23 reprinted in ibid., pp. 5–15.

66. Statement by the Algerian representative during the 28th meeting, ibid., p. 66, paragraph 2.

67. Statement by the American representative during the 28th meeting, ibid., p. 68, paragraph 11.

68. Ibid., p. 5, paragraph 16.

69. Ibid., p. 16, paragraph 57.

70. Statement by the representative of the USSR during the 29th meeting, ibid., p. 81, paragraph 72.

71. Statement by the representative from the P.L.O. during the 47th meeting, A/C.6/33/SR.47, paragraph 7.

72. Ibid., paragraph 9.

73. A/C.6/33/L.5 reprinted in A/33/385, paragraph 8.

74. Reprinted in A/34/39, pp. 1–2.

75. A/33/557.

76. A/34/39, p. 7, paragraph 19.

77. Ibid., p. 6, paragraph 18.

78. Ibid., pp. 7–8, paragraph 22.

79. Ibid., p. 8, paragraph 24.

80. Ibid., p. 8, paragraph 26.

81. A/AC.188/WG II/CRP.13 reprinted in ibid., p. 23.

82. Ibid., p. 4, paragraph 11.

83. Ibid., p. 22, paragraph 89. The proposed convention is reprinted on pp. 23–29.

84. An incident is considered to contain an international element if either the hostage-takers or the hostages are foreign nationals, the demands are focused on a foreign government, or the location of the incident involved a foreign embassy, consulate, or international organization.

# Proposals for Government and International Responses to Terrorism

Paul Wilkinson

University of Aberdeen

## I. Response at the National Level

### Introduction

The liberal state tough-line approach means combining harsh and effective temporary measures to isolate and eliminate terrorist cells, their leaders, and their logistic support, with the maintenance of liberal democracy, a vigorous political life of participation, debate and reform within the framework of the law. The key to this approach is not panic repression and over-reaction, which in any case play into the hands of terrorists, but a consistent policy of maximizing the risk of punishment run by the terrorists and minimizing their potential rewards. There are some historical examples of the effectiveness of this approach.

After France had suffered what is dubbed the "Dynamite Decade" of bomb outrages in the 1890s, the government used the weapon of *les lois scélérates*. These laws were deliberately aimed at suppressing anarchist movements and journals and even made it an offence to apologize for anarchist acts of violence. Despite the predictable outcry these measures caused in anarchist circles, there can be no doubt that they effectively snuffed out the anarchist terrorism that had mushroomed in the nineties. And, though the punishments meted out to convicted anarchists were harsh, it is also clear that the democratic institutions and processes of the French Third Republic managed to survive intact.

Again, there is the case of the newly independent Irish Free State confronted by the rebellion of the Irregulars who opposed the Treaty with Britain. The Free State government adopted emergency powers to deal with the terrorist and guerrilla campaign of the Irregulars between November 1922 and May 1923, setting up special military courts with the power to inflict the death penalty. In six months of the civil war almost twice as many Irregular prisoners were executed as the number of prisoners the British had executed between 1916 and 1921. These draconian measures certainly assisted the Free State government in restoring order: by May 24, 1923 the leaders of the Irregulars had conceded military defeat.

However, even when the tough-line approach has eliminated a specific threat to the security of the state or to law and order by destroying active terrorist cells, there will generally be passive sympathizers who remain. Indeed, part of the price we pay for the survival of democracy is the freedom of ideas. Hence, in a working liberal democracy it is both dangerous and naive to hope "to destroy a subversive movement utterly."[1]

To counter terrorism effectively the tough-line approach involves waging two kinds of war: a military-security war to contain and reduce terrorist violence, and a political and psychological war to secure the popular consent and support which must be the basis of any effective modern democratic government. It is fallacious to assume that terrorists need mass support before they can perpetrate murder and destruction: as we have already observed, many contemporary terrorist groups are numerically tiny. Yet it is important for the success of antiterrorist operations that popular support for the terrorists should remain limited to a minority—indeed that they be as isolated as possible from the general population.

To be successful this strategy demands a unified control of all counterinsurgency operations, an intelligence service of the highest quality, adequate security forces possessing the full range of counterinsurgency skills and complete loyalty to the government, and last but not least enormous reserves of patience and determination.[2]

There are rarely any easy victories over terrorism. The characteristic features of political terrorism, its undeclared and clandestine nature and its employment by desperate fanatics already *hors la loi*, imply a struggle of attrition constantly erupting into murder and disruption. Moreover, the terrorists know that security forces in a liberal state are forced to operate at dangerous mid-levels of coerciveness. Judicial restraints and civil control prevent the security forces from deploying their full strength and firepower. No doubt this is inevitable and desirable in a liberal democracy, but it does mean that the tasks of countering terrorism and urban guerrilla war in a democracy are enormously complex and demanding. We must now consider them in more detail.

## Anti-Terrorist Measures

*Some Ground Rules.* It is possible to draw from the recent experience of low-intensity and counterinsurgency operations certain basic ground rules which should be followed by liberal democracies taking a tough line against terrorism.

1. The democratically elected government must proclaim a determination to uphold the rule of law and constitutional authority, and must demonstrate this political will in its actions.
2. There must be no resort to general indiscriminate repression. The government must show that its measures against terrorism are solely directed at quelling the terrorists and their active collaborators and at defending society against the terrorists. A slide into general repression would destroy individual liberties and political democracy and may indeed bring about a ruthless dictatorship even more implacable than the terrorism the repression was supposed to destroy. Moreover, repressive over-reaction plays into the hands of terrorists by giving credence to the revolutionaries' claim that liberal democracy is a sham or a chimera, and it enables them to pose as defenders of the people.
3. The government must be seen to be doing all in its power to defend the life and limb of citizens. This is a vital prerequisite for public

confidence and cooperation. If it is lacking, private armies and vigilante groups will tend to proliferate and will exacerbate civil violence.

4. There must be a clearcut and consistent policy of refusing to make any concessions to terrorist blackmail. If the terrorist weapon can be shown to pay off against a particular government, then that government and its political moderates will find their power and authority undermined. There is abundant evidence that weakness and concession provoke a rapid emulation of terrorism by other groups and a dramatic escalation in the price of blackmail demands.

5. All aspects of the antiterrorist policy and operations should be under the overall control of the civil authorities and, hence, democratically accountable.

6. Special Powers, which may become necessary to deal with a terrorist emergency, should be approved by the legislature only for a fixed and limited period. The maximum should be six months, subject to the legislature's right to revoke or renew the Special Powers should circumstances require. Emergency measures should be clearly and simply drafted, published as widely as possible, and administered impartially.

7. Sudden vacillations in security policy should be avoided; they tend to undermine public confidence and encourage the terrorists to exploit rifts in the government and its security forces.

8. Loyal community leaders, officials, and personnel at all levels of government and security forces must be accorded full backing by the civil authorities.

9. No deals should be made with terrorist organizations behind the backs of the elected politicians.

10. The government should not engage in dialogue and negotiation with groups which are actively engaged in promoting, committing, or supporting terrorism. To do so only lends the terrorists publicity, status, and, worst of all, a spurious respectability.

11. Terrorist propaganda and defamation should be countered by full and clear official statements of the government's objectives, policies, and problems.

12. The government and security forces must conduct all antiterrorist operations within the law. They should do all in their power to ensure

that the normal legal processes are maintained, and that those charged with terrorist offences are brought to trial before the courts of law.

13. Terrorists imprisoned for crimes committed for professedly political motives should be treated in the same manner as ordinary criminals. Concessions of special status and other privileges tend to erode respect for the impartiality of the law, arouse false hopes of an amnesty, and impose extra strains on the penal system.

14. It is a vital principle that liberal democratic governments should not allow their concern with countering terrorism, even in a serious emergency, to deflect them from their responsibilities for the social and economic welfare of the community. Liberal democratic governments must, by definition, be grounded in the broad consent of the governed. They are inherently reformist and ameliorative; it is their citizens' natural and legitimate expectation that their representatives and ministers will respond constructively to the expressed needs and grievances of the people. The business of attending to the public welfare must go on. It is of course true that this is one of the greater inner strengths of liberal democracy and, incidentally, one reason why its citizens constitute such a hostile "sea" for the terrorist to swim in.

It would be the height of folly for a liberal democracy faced with a terrorist emergency to halt its work of amelioration and reform. On the contrary, everything possible should be done to prevent the serious disruption and paralysis of social and economic life so ardently sought by the terrorists. Yet, the liberal democratic government should not, on any account, conceded a reform or change of policy under terrorist duress. Such grave acts of weakness would only breed contempt for the normal political processes and for the law.

I must emphasize that the above general principles are not meant to be comprehensive. Much qualification and elaboration will be needed to relate these ground rules to the actual problems of conducting antiterrorist operations. Nevertheless, I do believe that these broad principles embody some of the major lessons that have been learned from antiterrorist campaigns of the past. It is now necessary to survey the strategy, tactics, measures, and resources of antiterrorist operations and to identify some of the more valuable forms of international response.

*The "Two Wars" Strategy.* The so-called "two-war" or "two-front" strategy was developed primarily by counterinsurgency specialists engaged in countering the "people's wars" of South-East Asia in the 1950s and 1960s. It is true that these conflicts involved a mixture of high and low intensity, and conventional and unconventional warfare. Terrorism, both rural and urban, was only part of the tactics of revolutionary warfare experienced in Malaya and Indo-China. Nevertheless, while there are enormous differences between these conflicts and contemporary terrorism within liberal democracies, the "two-war" strategic doctrine is still broadly applicable to low-intensity operations in heavily industrialized and urbanized societies.

The doctrine prescribes the harmonization of two distinctive kinds of campaign by the counterinsurgency forces:

(1) the military and security war to identify, isolate, and destroy the revolutionary forces, their leaders, logistic support, and lines of communication;
(2) the political, ideological, and psychological war to sustain and strengthen the base of popular support behind the government and hence to render the terrorists politically isolated and vulnerable.

Terrorists are always ready to exploit genuine grievances and profound social problems for their own revolutionary purposes. Naturally, governments are in a much stronger position if they can show some bona fide successes in tackling these socioeconomic problems. And terrorists invest considerable effort in the propaganda work of their political wings. Where the terrorist organization proper is proscribed, front organizations are used for this work. Governments must effectively counter the barrage of terrorist propaganda and defamation if the counterinsurgency campaign is to have any hope of success.

We need to identify and destroy the terrorist propaganda bases that are active in our communities. I am not suggesting that if you destroy those, you destroy the whole caboodle. The Soviet apparatus would still remain, operating on all cylinders, and so would the East European proxies. But there are groups busily engaged in propaganda and recruitment in most Western capitals. They are very important to the terrorist movement because you cannot hope to lead anything like an ethnic separatist or class-revolutionary movement without some of the constituents you are claiming to represent at least in your leadership committee and actually running the cells. You cannot run a movement which claims to be "liberating" Italy or "conquering Japanese imperialism" if you don't even have some platform in the country you are claiming to be liberating. In other words, it is very important that the propaganda and recruitment setups of terrorist organizations within democratic societies should be put out of business.

Where do we look for these? Publishing organizations and journals are often a sort of cover for this type of activity. There are also certain danger spots within the university systems. Now I am not suggesting for a moment that we close down certain universities. What I *am* suggesting is that we should know, and most of us can identify very easily if we do not know already, those university departments and those *individuals* in departments who are carrying out tasks for terrorist organizations as propagandists, as agents, and as recruiters. And they are the *key* initial point of entry for most active terrorists. It is the point at which most impressionable young people with some sort of political malleability and utopian enthusiasm may be mobilized by extremely ruthless people determined to keep the numbers of their terrorist organization up. Remember they are losing some all the time. Some are put in jail. Others defect or just run away. Thus they need to have this constant flow of recruits.

If you could stop the flow of recruits into the terrorist organizations, you could prevent much of the violence and damage done to society later on and you would have saved many young people. One might save many young people from the fate of becoming pawns of a terrorist organization, from becoming exploited by them. For indeed many are exploited. Many do not really want to stay in the movement. Some of them are trying to get out. It is hard for them because once the terrorists have got you, they use terror to keep you and the threat against your family or against your own life is enough to keep the average man or woman in the organization.

So therefore it is important for us to try and do two things:

 (i) locate those centers of recruitment and cut off the flow of recruits before the damage is done; and
 (ii) find ways of helping terrorists to leave their movements, and to become rehabilitated as constructive members of society.

In democracies our government and intelligence agencies should make a priority of examining the development of university bases of recruitment by the terrorist organizations operating in their region. And they should have close liaison with the academic authorities known to be sympathetic to the task of protecting free societies in order to elicit their cooperation in avoiding recruiting to university staff people who are likely to act as terrorist agents and propagandists. Its an ongoing business. As one man or woman is not given tenure, another one comes along who looks all right, who has been fitted out with all the appropriate qualifications, but really is primarily working for a terrorist organization. Thus, part of the war against terrorism has to be fought out in the seminar and lecture rooms of the universities of the Western world; it is literally a struggle for the souls of the young. The Italian police have discovered this reality, rather late in the day. We need to apply the lessons about our moral and spiritual defenses against terrorism in all the Western democracies.

Of course, political will and propaganda cannot win the whole war against terrorism on their own. Battles on the military, security, and political fronts all need to be won. But there are two key lessons I think we can draw. You cannot win against terror by military methods alone, except perhaps in a totalitarian state that none of us would want to live in. And you cannot win *solely* by better propaganda. Charles Roetter, in *Psychological Warfare*, wrote, "Propaganda is no substitute for victory. It cannot unmake defeats. It can help prepare the way for the former and speed its coming: and it can mitigate the impact of the latter. It cannot act in isolation. To be effective, it must be closely related to events."

That is rather a wise comment and it does apply very much to the terrorist situation. The gravest danger of all, in situations of severe and protracted challenge by terrorists, is that the moral integrity, will, and loyalty of a democracy may become eroded under the impact of general cynicism, the blind pursuit of self-interest by powerful groups, such as the oil companies unprepared to take any strong measures against terrorism for fear of upsetting the Arabs, or the media allowing a voracious appetite for sensationalism to influence them in letting forces of law and order suffer consequences of media irresponsibility.

Any liberal state heavily demoralized and under strain from inflation and recession could be pushed into destroying itself without a shot being fired. (I leave you to guess which countries I have in mind as being the most likely to suffer that fate.) If one injects the element of terrorism and the probable disorganization that could be provoked by simultaneous terrorist attacks in many parts of a democratic state, it does not take a great effort of imagination to envisage a scenario of political collapse. It is essential for us to see terrorism in the context of a worsening climate of conflict. It may be only one element, but in certain key crises it may be the decisive catalyst for the destruction of democracy. A democratic system that is undefeated at the ballot box can still be destroyed by its failure to defend itself against determined attack by the enemy within the gates. Terrorism may well be the Trojan Horse.

*Police as Intelligence Agents.* An intelligence service of the highest quality is clearly a vital prerequisite for any effective counterinsurgency campaign. It is absolutely crucial for combatting terrorist bombings and assassinations which present difficulties of a rather different order from the problems of full-scale guerrilla war. The archetypal terrorist organization is numerically tiny and based on a structure of cells or firing groups, each consisting of three or four individuals. These generally exercise a fair degree of operational independence and initiative, and are obsessively concerned with the security of their organization and lines of communication. Usually only one member of each cell is fully acquainted with the group's links with other echelons and with the terrorist directorate.

Experienced terrorists develop sophisticated "cover" to protect themselves against detection and infiltration. They are adept at disappearing into the shadows of the urban and suburban environment. They increasingly tend to acquire the funds and resources necessary to shift their bases between cities and across frontiers. Modern internationally-based terrorist organizations take full advantage of the mobility afforded by air travel, and are adroit at shifting their bases of operations when things become too hot for them.

For all these reasons the police are the most appropriate intelligence agency for combatting terrorism. I do not share General Kitson's view[3] that intelligence gathering should be primarily an Army responsibility. It is true that in the special circumstances of the troubles in Ulster police effectiveness has been somewhat vitiated by the sectarian conflict. But in most Western states the police Special Branch or its equivalent has enormous advantages over the military in the investigation and prevention of terrorist crimes.

They have firm roots in the local communities and possess an invaluable "bank" of data on both extremist and criminal groups. Moreover, the Army does not possess the manpower, time, or police training to duplicate the work of the police forces. Defense chiefs have to make their primary concern the meeting of external defense obligations, and they generally prefer to husband their intelligence services for use in operations in which the Army is militarily involved.

Police in Western democracies have learned many valuable lessons from their recent experience of terrorism. There have been three main trends in this development:

(1) improvements in techniques of intelligence gathering, infiltration and surveillance, and in data computerization. By these means background information can be more readily developed into contact information;
(2) improvements in the machinery for coordination of antiterrorist operations at the national level; and
(3) greater international cooperation, and exchange of data on international terrorism on a regular basis.

*The Army's Role.* What should be the role of the Army in countering terrorism? Even in the initial phases of a terrorist campaign, it can provide invaluable aid to the civil power. Bomb disposal, sharpshooting, and training and testing in new techniques and weaponry are some obvious roles in which military expertise may be invaluable. But I believe that the Army should be handed the overall task of maintaining internal security and order only as a last resort; troops should be brought in when it is obvious that the civil power is unable to cope and that there is a very real risk of civil war. If they are given this task, they should be given a clear remit and briefing on their role by the civil authorities, and they should be withdrawn as soon as the level of violence has dropped to a level at which the police can act effectively.

There are a number of dangers involved in deploying the Army in a major internal terrorist emergency role which need be constantly borne in mind:

(1) an unnecessarily high military profile may serve to escalate the level of violence by polarizing pro- and antigovernment elements in the community;

(2) there is a constant risk that a repressive over-reaction or a minor error of judgment by the military may trigger further civil violence. Internal security duties inevitably impose considerable strains on the soldiers who are made well aware of the hostility of certain sections of the community toward them;

(3) antiterrorist and internal security duties absorb considerable manpower and involved diverting highly trained military technicians from their primary NATO and external defense roles;

(4) there is a risk that the civil power may become overdependent upon the Army's presence, and there may be a consequent lack of urgency in preparing the civil police for gradually reshouldering the internal security responsibility.

Britain is fortunate in having an Army steeped in democratic ethos. They have shown enormous skill, courage, and patience in carrying out a number of extraordinarily difficult counterinsurgency tasks around the world since 1945. Their loyalty in carrying out their instructions from the civil government has never been put in question. In Northern Ireland it is doubtful whether any other army could have performed the internal security role with such humanity, restraint, and effectiveness.

It would be naive to assume that all liberal democracies are as fortunate. It is notorious that many armies, particularly conscript armies, have been infiltrated and subverted by extremist organizations of left and right. Both the Italian and French Armies have had to weed out left-wing activists who were undermining military discipline.

The recent history of Greece affords a vivid demonstration of the consequences of widespread disaffection and political subversion within the armed forces. It is a warning that no liberal democracy can afford to ignore, for loyal and disciplined armed forces are the last line of defense for democracies in crisis.

*Mobilizing the Public.* Yet there are many other valuable lines of defense open to liberal democracies before the Army is put to the ultimate test of preserving the state. The ordinary, loyal, and decent citizens are themselves a priceless asset in combatting terrorism if only they can be mobilized to help the government and security forces. One way of doing this is to enroll large numbers of ablebodied men into the police reserves. One is aware that these auxiliaries are treated with some disdain by the professionals, and that there is considerable resistance in some quarters to extending the police reserve. Nevertheless, when so many of our major city police forces are below efficient strength a large injection of police reserve manpower could considerably ease the situation.

Police reserves would have an obvious benefit for the effective conduct of antiterrorist operations. Full-time and specialist-trained officers would be freed from more routine duties and more time and manpower could be devoted to combatting terrorist crime. Moreover, there is no reason why police reserves could not adequately perform many of the extra duties of patrols, searches, and vehicle checks that may be necessitated by a terrorist emergency. The writer strongly recommends that measures to increase the police reserves be given urgent consideration.

Another valuable way of mobilizing public assistance against terrorism is through a concerted program of public information and education about how to recognize bombs and terrorist weapons, the procedure to be adopted when a suspicious object is sighted, the kind of information that might be valuable to the police, the speediest method of communication with the antiterrorist squad, and so forth. There should also be much more use of television, radio, and public advertisement to convey this essential information. There is a rich fund of experience from Ulster and elsewhere concerning the most effective methods of mobilizing the public behind an antiterrorist campaign.

The security authorities should also take care to brief special groups such as property owners in areas under attack and businessmen concerning the particular terrorist hazards that they are most likely to confront, and to give special advice on appropriate countermeasures. It is to be hoped that the police in British cities have already held such consultations with owners of premises and places of entertainment. The police should also make a regular practice of informing regional hospital authorities of the kind of emergency situations that are likely to arise through terrorist attacks. This task of public education and mobilization is just as vital to the task of saving lives as the formulation of contingency plans for military and police action.

One general aim of such measures should be to make the public far more security conscious. Members of the public must be constantly vigilant for suspicious objects or activities in the environs of buildings, for signs of tampering with vehicles, and for unattended bags and parcels. Gunsmiths and commercial suppliers of chemicals and explosives should, as a matter of routine, check that their customers are bona fide. Any irregular transactions or unaccountable losses should be immediately reported to the police. The eyes and ears of the security forces must be the citizens.

Indeed, without the fullest public cooperation special preventive measures against terrorism are bound to fail. Take, for example, the matter of storage of detonators and explosive substances for industrial purposes. It would do no earthly good for the government to bring in a new Act to impose severe penalties for failing to keep explosive stores fully secure if the actual workers and managers involved in their industrial use still failed to observe the minimal rules of security. Police are generally called in only when there is an explosives or weapons theft, i.e., when it is probably too late. Truly preventive action against terrorism demands the fullest cooperation of every member of the public.

*Special Powers: Detention.* What should be the role of Special Powers in a terrorist emergency? And which have been shown to be the most effective? Much nonsense is uttered equating the use of Special Powers with the abandonment of political democracy. Of course, the terrorists' political propaganda eagerly seizes upon any crude and confused emotionalism about basic rights being "trampled on" and uses it to foster its myth of repression. Such powers do represent a partial curtailment or restriction of the normal freedoms of a peaceful democracy, but in a liberal state they are, by definition, a temporary expedient to be used only as an ultimate weapon to help save democracy from its enemies within.

Proscription of terrorist organizations, making membership of such groups illegal, normally results in driving the groups underground, making police surveillance more difficult. However, this disadvantage may be considerably outweighed by the gain in public morale and support for the government. It is widely felt to be intolerable that a terrorist organization should flaunt itself publicly while the tally of victims of its atrocities rises. Moreover, proscription does curtail open recruitment and fund raising. Temporary bans on marches and demonstrations may considerably assist in reducing the level of violence and tension, and can free security forces from the thankless tasks of riot control.

The most controversial Special Powers are those which extend police powers of detention without trial. This is clearly a suspension of habeas corpus, yet it must be recognized that in a serious emergency the normal judicial processes may simply be unable to function. They can break down because of terrorization and intimidation of witnesses, juries, and lawyers. The police may be totally hamstrung in their attempts to get a man known to be guilty actually convicted and sentenced by a court of law. Are they then to return him to society to continue his systematic murder? This historical evidence in Ulster shows clearly that the level of violence actually increases with each wave of detainee releases. Detention without trial is a security source that government cannot afford to discard lightly in a severe terrorist emergency situation. However, if detention without trial is used it is essential that it should be subject to automatic periodic review by an impartial judicial tribunal.

Less controversial, but also of proven value to the security forces, is the power to exclude and deport aliens suspected of terrorist activities. In certain states (for example, Eire) use has also been made of powers to ban terrorist organizations and their propaganda from the media. This denial of a public platform certainly hits the terrorists hard; they delude themselves if they believe that their "underground" and informal propaganda is just as effective as the established media. The FLQ in Québec in October 1970 were so desperate for publicity that they actually made the broadcasting of their manifesto a condition for negotiating the release of their kidnap victim, James Cross.

## II. Response at the International Level

### *Introduction*

Substantial progress has been made in the field of international cooperation in Western Europe, but this has not sufficed to prevent this region from experiencing a higher proportion of terrorist attacks than any other. The EEC Ministers of the Interior and the police forces and intelligence services of the member states have since 1976 developed regular machinery for discussion and practical multilateral cooperation.

But the most ambitious attempt at European cooperation at the judicial level is the Council of Europe Convention on the Suppression of Terrorism, which 17 out of 19 Council of Europe member states signed in January 1977, when the Convention was opened for signature.[4]

## *"Political" Offences Loophole*

The Convention provides, in effect, that all ratifying states will exclude the whole range of major terrorist offences, such as assassinations, hostage taking, bomb attacks, and hijacking, from the political offence exception clauses that had previously been used to justify refusal of extradition, in other words, to ensure that all contracting states would treat such offences as common crimes. In cases where, because of some technical or constitutional difficulty, a contracting state is unable to carry out extradition, the Convention obliges the authorities to bring the suspect to trial before their own courts. Mutual assistance in criminal investigation of such offences is also made mandatory.

However, the admirable intentions of this Convention have been seriously obstructed by two major shortcomings. First, a possible escape clause was inserted into the Convention permitting a contracting state to reserve the right to regard a certain offence as political, and hence to withhold extradition.

Second, the process of ratification has been disgracefully slow despite the speedy signature of the Convention in January 1977. France and Belgium, for example, have been reluctant to ratify on the grounds that they are constitutionally committed to guarantee the right of political asylum. (It seems odd that, despite all the careful safeguards in the Convention, they are still unprepared to exclude those charged with serious crimes of terrorism from this right.) And by late 1980 only ten member states had completed ratification (Sweden, Austria, West Germany, Denmark, Great Britain, Iceland, Cyprus, Spain, Luxembourg, and Norway). An *espace judiciaire européen*   (a European judicial zone) seemed, to say the least, premature.

Two other recent moves to improve international cooperation against terrorism are worth mentioning. At their Bonn summit meeting of July 1978, the Heads of Government of Canada, France, Italy, Japan, the United Kingdom, the United States, and West Germany came out with a firm collective statement promising sanctions against states aiding and abetting aircraft hijacking. Their communiqué stated:

> In cases where a country refuses the extradition or prosecution of those who have hijacked an aircraft, or refuses to return it, the Heads of State or government are additionally resolved that they will take immediate action to cease all flights to that country. At the same time their governments will

initiate action to halt all incoming flights from that country or from any country, by the airlines of the country concerned.

Experts met in August 1978 to discuss the practicalities of implementing this agreement. There is every reason to welcome this firm stand in favor of sanctions by the major Western states, for it may exert a continuing deterrent effect against rogue states which have, in the past, helped to encourage hijacking. However, a cynic might note that aircraft hijacking was no longer the major terrorist threat by July 1978; action had really been needed in 1969–73 when the menace was at its peak.

Finally, there was an encouragingly positive meeting of the EEC Ministers of Justice in early October 1978 who proposed a Convention similar to the Council of Europe Convention on the Suppression of Terrorism for use between all the nine EEC states, again based on the *aut dedere aut punire* principle. This would enable states (such as Ireland) which claim to have constitutional difficulties over extradition to at least guarantee that terrorist suspects will be brought to trial in their country of origin or residence, but sadly France will not allow this agreement to be enforced.

## Intelligence and Police Cooperation

One of the most important aspects of Western cooperation is the strengthening of the machinery for multilateral police and intelligence cooperation, and this has generally progressed far more rapidly than political and judicial cooperation. It takes place at five different levels:

1. Interpol (the International Criminal Police Organization) is under its constitution strictly confined to dealing with ordinary law crimes, but as this covers many terrorist acts the organization has had some value in acting as a clearing house for information. For instance, in July 1976 Athens police were able to identify a West German terrorist, Rolf Pohle, with the aid of the Interpol photos, and detain him.
2. NATO has developed a valuable system for the exchange of intelligence concerning terrorist weapons, personnel, and techniques, which has been of great assistance to member states.
3. Joint training visits and exchanges of security personnel are now well established among the EEC and NATO countries.

4. Bilateral cooperation has been provided on an ad hoc basis at the request of governments. Thus, British SAS personnel, techniques, and weapons have been made available to support Dutch and West German counterterrorist operations. And the West German computer bank of data on terrorists has been used in the fight against terrorism in Italy and elsewhere.

5. There is a permanent structure of police cooperation between EEC member states of particular value in combatting cross-border terrorism.

## Bilateral Cooperation

It is not generally realized that one of the most effective methods of cooperation against terrorism takes the form of bilateral agreements between neighboring states. A notable instance of this occurred in the U.S.–Cuba Hijack Pact of February 1973, in which both governments agreed to return hijacked aircraft, crews, passengers, and hijackers. It is true that Cuba insisted on a caveat enabling her to refuse to return terrorists affiliated to a national liberation movement recognized by Cuba. But as most hijackers who sought sanctuary in Cuba from the United States were criminals or psychopaths, this clause did not undermine the effectiveness of the agreement. Moreover, even though Cuba refused formally to renew the agreement, following the blowing-up of a Cuban airliner by anti-Castro exiles in October 1976, the fact is that Cuba has continued to operate in the spirit of the Pact, and it undoubtedly contributed to the temporary defeat of the hijacking plague that afflicted the United States between 1970 and 1972.

An even more unlikely example of partnership was the cooperation between Somalia and West Germany in the GSG-9 (Grenzschutzgruppen 9—the German antiterrorist unit) operation to rescue the Lufthansa hostages at Mogadishu. After all, Somalia was a Marxist regime which had previously been used as a base by terrorists organizing the Air France hijack to Entebbe. Yet, encouraged by the prospect of economic assistance, the new state rendered valuable service by allowing in the German rescue squad.

If such diverse political systems can cooperate profitably, surely it should not be beyond the power of the Western European states to improve their own bilateral security cooperation? There is some encouraging recent evidence that this is being developed in two areas particularly hard-hit by terrorist violence over the past decade: the Basque region and Northern Ireland. In January 1979 France abolished refugee status for Spanish nationals in France, on the sensible ground that Spain, as a democracy, no longer had political refugees. Almost simultaneously 13 Spanish Basques living near the Spanish border were banished to the remote Hautes-Alpes in eastern France. This was France's very positive response to Spanish government demands for more vigorous cooperation to stamp out terrorism.

French border country has long been regarded as a valuable sanctuary and launching-point for ETA terrorism, and the new measures will do much to assist the Spanish authorities' counterterrorist drive. France itself has a strong interest in helping to combat ETA terrorism, for the recent assassinations in France of two Basque leaders in revenge attacks were an unpleasant warning of the way in which ETA terrorism could spill over the frontier.

In the wake of the Provisional IRA massacres at Warrenpoint and Mullaghmore on August Bank Holiday Monday 1979[5] the governments of the Irish Republic and the United Kingdom have held a series of meetings to discuss closer security cooperation. The measures agreed on in the talks held in September and October are an excellent practical illustration of cooperation between two parliamentary democracies to curb a terrorist campaign of murder which threatens them both. The new measures, including improved border cooperation, are a bold and imaginative effort to curb terrorism which is now the major obstacle to a lasting peace and reconciliation in Ireland.

### Extradition Problems

If the international community is to minimize the rewards of terrorism and maximize its risks and costs it must be seen to be possible to bring terrorist suspects to justice even when they slip across frontiers. But extradition is a highly complex and unpredictable process. Many states do not have extradition agreements and where these do exist they frequently exclude political offences—the term "political" is often very liberally construed. Differences in criminal codes, procedures, and judicial traditions also have to be taken into account. Often the extradition procedures becomes highly protracted, owing to difficulties in obtaining evidence and witnesses from abroad. In the British extradition hearings in the case of Astrid Proll in 1978/79 there was a further complication—a dispute over nationality. (Despite delays and difficulties, however, Astrid Proll was eventually extradited to West Germany where she was charged with attempted murder of two policemen and other crimes, but was later released.)

Extradition proceedings succeed in the cases of only a small minority of terrorist suspects. Between January 1960 and June 1976, 20 states requested extradition of 78 hijackers but this was granted in only five cases, though 42 of the offenders were prosecuted by the recipient state. Small wonder that in many cases states use deportation as a form of "disguised extradition" and as this is a civil—as opposed to criminal—proceeding it does not afford the individual the same opportunities to present his or her own case. However, deportation merely shifts the problem to another state, and does not ensure that a suspected terrorist is brought to justice. On all these grounds this method ought not to be encouraged. A far more desirable course is for states to attempt to standardize their criminal codes and procedures to facilitate the application of the "extradite or prosecute" principle.

Nor is it the case that states can always be depended upon to honor the letter or spirit of their extradition agreements. A government which fears a retaliatory attack by terrorists or which is subject to blackmail by, say, the Arab oil weapon, may well decide that "national interest" demands that they let a suspect go free. A notorious case occurred in January 1977, when Abu Daoud, suspected of involvement in the planning of the Munich massacre, was arrested in Paris on an Interpol warrant issued by the West German police. Israel immediately announced that it would request Daoud's extradition, on the ground that he was to be charged with the murder of Israeli citizens. A Paris court rejected attempts to extradite him, and he was allowed to travel to Algeria. The West German authorities expressed surprise and regret at this decision, and the international community drew the conclusion that the French government had put its desire for remunerative new commercial agreements with Arab states before its obligations to combat international terrorism.

## Problems of Establishing a European Judicial Area

The first problem to consider is what is meant by a "European judicial area"? President Giscard d'Estaing and spokesmen for the French government have been extremely vague. The concept of an *espace judiciaire européen,* first floated in 1978, has an impressive resonance, with its overtones of comprehensiveness and enforceability. But what precisely is the intention? The establishment of a common jurisdiction, legal code, and legal process for crimes of terrorism throughout the European democracies? The setting up of a European Court for all cases of terrorist crimes? Or merely the ratification and implementation of extradition treaties and the European conventions on the suppression of terrorism?

Nation-states have traditionally clutched very tightly to their monopoly of internal legal sovereignty. There are certainly no current indications that they are now more willing even to consider relaxing this hold. It seems extremely unlikely that even the European Community states would be ready to pool their sovereignty in sensitive matters crucially affecting national security, the suppression of crime, and maintenance of law and order. Thus the pooling of sovereignty and the establishment of some common legal code and judicial process to deal with terrorist crimes throughout democratic Europe can be ruled out as an impracticable option. Such developments would only appear feasible if, at some future date, European countries were to unite under a federal government. While our countries remain independent nation-states, governments will continue to regard these matters as the exclusive responsibility of national governments.

This state of affairs does not, of course, preclude improvements in international judicial, police, and intelligence cooperation. Yet if we examine progress to date in the most ambitious attempt at international cooperation, the European Convention on the Suppression of Terrorism, for which the Council of Europe must take full credit, it is all too evident that there are severe obstacles.

On the face of it this may seem hard to understand. After all, the European democracies are geographically concentrated, many with common frontiers and long histories of bilateral contact and cooperation. Their legal, political, and economic systems have much in common. And, of course, the establishment of the European Economic Community might well encourage one to believe that some degree of legal and political integration may, after all, be possible. More to the point, all our countries have a common problem in curbing the high incidence of domestic and international terrorism.

No one should doubt the urgency of the problem for the European countries. Over 50 percent of the world's internationally linked terrorist incidents in 1979 occurred in NATO Europe, i.e., 783 out of a total of 1550 incidents. This was *over double* the figure for NATO Europe incidents in the previous year (357).

Moreover, the very nature of modern international terrorism demands effective international response. Terrorists shift their bases and their operations rapidly from capital to capital. They crisscross frontiers to evade detection. They collaborate with fraternal groups and sympathizers abroad, and often rely on foreign states and movements for weapons, cash, training, and other valuable forms of support.

Given the urgent need for international cooperation, how does one explain the snail's pace of the ratification process of the European Convention? Why is it that even the modest approach of applying the principle *aut dedere aut punire* (extradite or punish) has been more honored in the breach?

The major difficulty is that each state is proud of its own national laws and traditions. National publics may often criticize aspects of their own systems, and demand reforms in the law, but they are not sympathetic to the idea that their own system should have to change in order to accommodate to some supranational or intergovernmental design.

In addition to national differences and national chauvinism, there is a considerable residue of popular mistrust and suspicion concerning the quality of their neighbors' political and legal systems. Sometimes this is rooted in an earlier history of conflict and the feeling that you can never really rely on professions of good faith and good will by the government of a former enemy. Often it is based on sheer xenophobia. A particularly glaring example of this type of prejudice emerged in a recent European Parliament debate on antiterrorism legislation!

A more intractable problem arises when one European government comes to the conclusion that the government of a neighboring state is actually shielding terrorists they wish to have extradited, or that neighboring states are delaying or obstructing the process of rendering *mutual assistance* as required under Article 8 of the European Convention.

In really serious cases of interstate disagreements—as, for instance, in the dealings between the Northern Ireland and Irish Republic judiciaries over the questioning of suspects and witnesses—the whole process of judicial and police cooperation can become jeopardized.

It was partly due to recognition of these profound problems that the drafters of the European Convention on the Suppression of Terrorism wisely allowed enormous flexibility. They were particularly concerned not to exclude from the Convention states that had a deep attachment to constitutional traditions or guarantees of political asylum. This is, of course, the rationale behind Article 13 of the Convention which permits any state:

> at the time of signature or when depositing its instrument of ratification, acceptance or approval, to declare that it reserves the right to refuse extradition in respect of any offence mentioned in Article 1 which it considers to be a political offence, an offence connected with a political offence or an offence inspired by political motives.

At first sight this Article of Reservation appears to negate the whole value of the Convention and its important core proposition that crimes of terrorism should be treated as serious common crimes.

There is no doubt that Article 13 does in a very fundamental sense contradict the basic philosophy of the Convention. It is a powerful testimony to the deep differences in constitutional and legal traditions to which I have already referred.

It became obvious, however, that there would be no chance of achieving a general European Convention on Terrorism without the inclusion of such a reservation clause. I was only one of many who argued strongly that the Convention was gravely weakened by this inherent contradiction.

However, it is also important to recognize that the Article of Reservation does not, in effect, totally undermine the Convention's efficacy. There is a crucial rider to the effect that when a State invokes Article 13 it has an obligation:

to take into due consideration, when evaluating the character of the offence, any particularly serious aspects of the offence, including:

a) that it created a collective danger to the life, physical integrity or liberty of persons; or
b) that it affected persons foreign to the motives behind it; or
c) that cruel or vicious means have been used in the commission of the offence.

On signature of the Convention, France, Italy, and Norway all declared their intention to invoke the Article of Reservation, (though in the case of France the declaration is couched in such cloudy and ambiguous terms that it implies that additional Reservations will be entered). Five states have invoked Article 13 when depositing ratification.

Now as I understand it, if and when all those states that entered the Reservation Article on signature do eventually ratify the Convention, they must honor their commitment under Article 13 and not allow the excuse of political motivation to exempt persons accused of what is clearly a terroristic crime from being extradited. Indeed it is the rider to Article 13 of the Convention which comes closest to defining the characteristics of a terroristic act of violence. Thus all is not lost.

In view of the fact that such grave difficulties were encountered in drawing up a Convention on Terrorism generally acceptable to the European democracies, and in the light of the painfully slow process of ratification and *implementation*, what possible hope is there for a more ambitious and all-embracing harmonization?

I have reluctantly concluded that the European Convention represents the *optimal mechanism* for European cooperation in the fight against terrorism, given the present condition of international relations. Rather than spending more time and effort in discussing fresh institutions or mechanisms we should pursue the more modest aim of making the existing machinery work effectively. Moreover, there is no doubt that recent efforts by the Council of Europe and the European Community toward a greater degree of convergence in the jurisdiction, legal codes, and judicial procedures of the European states could immeasurably assist in smoothing the path for closer judicial cooperation and an effective implementation of the Convention on the Suppression of Terrorism.

So far this paper has argued that President Giscard d'Estaing's con-

cept of an *espace judiciaire européen*,    however laudable its motivation, is neither clearly defined nor feasible, and that our energies would
be better spent on making the more modest, though still painfully
difficult, Convention machinery work.

But in my view there is another fundamental reason why it would be a
mistake for Europe to set off in search of the chimerical "European
judicial zone." Even if we were able to achieve such an agreement, and
as I have said I think this is extremely doubtful, it would not really tackle
the major and growing problem of the "spillover" into Europe's
capitals of international terrorism, much of it launched as a form of
proxy war by regimes, from the Middle East and other non-European
areas. Cities such as Paris, London, Vienna, Athens, and Rome have
in recent years become the favorite killing grounds of terroristic groups
and the hired assassins of dictatorial regimes. European governments
are rightly worried about the growing toll of diplomats, emigrés, and
ex-political leaders who have become victims of such attacks; they are
naturally even more concerned about the growing number of their own
citizens—policemen and members of the general public—whose lives
are being put at risk in these incidents.

The action urgently required to counter this "spillover" of terrorism
from beyond Europe's borders has little or nothing to do with the debate
on the European judicial area. What is called for is a determined and
united stand by all democratic governments against the abuses of diplomatic privileges and flagrant sponsorship for the staging of terrorism,
by states such as Iran, Libya and Syria, wherever and whenever they
occur, and against whomsoever they are directed.

It is primarily the responsibility of each individual Western government to clean out the Augean stable of modern "diplomatic terrorism,"
and to ensure that grave breaches of the Vienna Convention (1961) on
diplomatic relations are not tolerated. It is their prerogative, when
necessary, to expel diplomats, to declare individuals *persona non grata*,
and, in extreme circumstances, to sever diplomatic relations. In my
view the European governments, both individually and collectively,
have been appallingly weak and irresponsible in failing to use these
powers. They have allowed international law to be contemptuously
defied by foreign states and nationals. They have all too often backed
down or turned a blind eye rather than put at risk some tempting export
contract or access to oil or other valuable commodities. Such pathetic

weakness inevitably invites further humiliations and further undermining of already fragile international laws and conventions.

A shameful recent example of weakness of this kind was the British Parliament's sabotaging of the trade sanctions arrangements against Iran, previously agreed to by the EEC foreign ministers. Iran has been guilty of the most outrageous violation of the international law of diplomacy in modern history. Their ''regime'' of religious fanatics has colluded with a group of ''students'' in abducting the entire U.S. diplomatic mission, and incarcerating them for over a year.

The Americans are Western Europeans' tried and trusted allies: they have saved Western Europe from tyranny twice in this century. They still provide the crucial military power to protect us from being overrun a third time. Yet there are powerful voices not only in the British Parliament but in all the West European states who are unwilling to give the Americans even the basic diplomatic and economic backing they deserve against this barbaric tin-pot regime of mad mullahs, wading in the blood of their executions. Thus the West European ''allies'' have not been prepared to sever diplomatic relations with Teheran. Iranian diplomats walk the streets of Western cities enjoying full immunity, protection, and privilege. (As supreme irony, in London the magnificent British SAS and Police actually demonstrated the quality of this protection by rescuing their embassy hostages!) How extraordinary that, despite all that the Iranians are doing to Americans, not a single European ally has had the courage to sever diplomatic relations with Teheran. How disgraceful that they had been too frightened of losing Iranian markets and oil supplies to freeze Iranian financial assets in European banks or to introduce a total ban on trade.

When acts of terrorism promoted by oil states provoke such a febrile response from European democracies, and international law and morality are trampled under foot, rhetoric about a European judicial zone against terrorism is bound to sound like a sick joke.

If the European states wish to do something more constructive about international cooperation against terrorism they could make a useful start by demanding an international conference to review the workings of the Vienna Convention on diplomatic relations, and by proposing new clauses to strengthen it and to tighten its enforcement. But I suspect they would rather muddle along, trying to make the best of the present system, and trying hard not to give too much offence to the susceptibilities of those pro-terrorist states possessing the potent blackmail weapons of oil and oil surpluses.

## A Coordinating Group?

There is also a real need to create a small international commission or specialist department, preferably under the aegis of the EEC, to coordinate Western cooperation against international terrorism. There is already a framework of regular meetings of European Ministers of the Interior, and for police coordination and intelligence sharing. Bilateral cooperation between police forces, intelligence services, and specialist antiterrorist units is far more advanced than collaboration at the judicial and political levels, but is at present conducted on a piecemeal basis.

A central coordinating antiterrorist cell of say half-a-dozen top security and intelligence experts, with adequate research and administrative support and access to all meetings of Community Ministers of the Interior and Justice and the intelligence and police chiefs of member states, could add immeasurably to the precision and quality of the international response. The new unit should provide expert analyses of intelligence data, assessment of responsibilities and threats, a continuing research and development backup, including work on the pooling of counterterrorist weaponry and technology, training and briefing services, and advice to ministers, police, and security services.

One of its most urgently needed contributions would be to provide coordinated contingency plans and crisis-management machinery when two or more member states are involved in an incident. Just imagine, for example, the confusion and panic that would have set in if, as so easily might have happened, diplomats of a number of different Western states had been abducted together with the Americans, in Iran. There is at present absolutely no proper coordinating mechanism to deal with such an eventuality. Yet with the growing number of sieges of diplomatic premises and the offices of international organizations and companies around the world, such "multinational" mass hostage-takings are increasingly likely. Indeed, early this year diplomatic representatives of a dozen different countries were seized in a terrorist attack at Bogotá.

It should also help to organize joint exercises in hostage rescue and other counterterrorist operations and supervise training of personnel of member states in hostage negotiation. This coordinating commission could also serve as a means to improve antiterrorist intelligence links between the EEC states and other democracies, such as the United States, Japan, Canada, and Australia. It could promote research in improved technologies of prevention and encourage higher standards of security education in government and industry.

It is no good looking to national officials, police, and intelligence services to take the initiative in establishing an international coordinating unit of this kind. They tend to be instinctively conservative and suspicious and jealous of their own monopolies of access to ministers and intelligence sources. The fact remains that more sophisticated international coordination especially for contingencies of the kind mentioned is urgently required.

It is up to the leading politicians with vision and a sense of the international realities to exert the necessary pressure to secure police and security coordination which matches the needs of the 1980s and 1990s.

## Hostage-Rescue Flying Squads

Finally, and once more taking into account the global context of modern international terrorism, I advocate the formation of special hostage-rescue commando units for every major region of the world. These might most usefully be established under the aegis of the regional organization (such as Organization of African Unity, Organization of American States, Association of South East Asian Nations, European Economic Community) or, if this proves impossible, under the UN on a similar basis to peacekeeping contingents. Such specialized units would be provided at the request of a government experiencing grave problems in coping with an international terrorist incident. It would be able to bring to bear on the situation all the latest techniques and technologies of siege management, hostage negotiation, and hostage rescue.

It would be a valuable and positive step if the Council of Europe could make a start in proposing a standby unit of the kind for Europe. If this proves successful it could then provide a model for other regions of the world.

## Guidelines for the Democracies' Response

If, as has been argued, effective action through world bodies is currently impracticable, what should the Western democracies do to counter the threat of international terrorism? As has already been made clear, this threat is largely directed toward the democratic societies of Western Europe and North America. What can we usefully do?

First and foremost, we should keep our democratic systems in good political and economic repair. In particular we should try to respond positively to the changing needs and demands of the populace, including protecting the rights of minorities. This requires balanced and effective structures of representative democracy at both the local and national level, with ultimate control by the elected bodies over the bureaucracy, armed forces, police, and security services, ensuring their full accountability. A sure sign of danger is the accretion of overweening power by officials or by specific agencies of the state.

An independent judiciary is a prerequisite for the maintenance of the rule of law and the constitution and a vital ally of the elected government and legislature in ensuring democratic control and accountability. In a terrorist situation it is essential that the authorities and security forces act entirely within the law. Extra-legal actions will only tend to undermine democratic legitimacy and destroy public confidence. Any breach of legality will be exploited by terrorist propagandists to show the hypocrisy of the claims by the government and the security forces to be acting in the name of the law, and to try to persuade waverers that the government is not worth supporting.

Operating outside the strict rule of law is thus not only morally wrong: it is likely to be counterproductive. In observing these legal constraints democratic governments must constantly make it clear that when terrorists are convicted and punished it is not because of their professed political beliefs but because they have committed serious criminal offences. Because the punishment is for criminal deeds and not for political motives or causes it would be totally wrong to accord jailed terrorists some "special status" as "political prisoners." Refusal to grant such status is entirely consistent with the philosophy of judicial control common to all the Western democracies, and is implicit in the terms of the European Convention on the Suppression of Terrorism which seeks to define certain terroristic offences as common crimes.[6]

It is also vital for democratic governments to strive for a sound and healthy economy, and it is in all their interests to cooperate more effectively in creating the right policies to deal with those now universal twin evils of Western economies—runaway inflation and high unemployment. In a climate of massive recession and industrial collapse it is inevitable that the fear and frustration generated among the working population will give rise to militant and violent confrontations. Economic chaos and collapse create a far greater danger of destabilization of democracy than the actions of a handful of terrorists are likely to cause. For it is in the conditions of major economic breakdown that the real threat of a wider escalation into internal war (in which terrorism would play merely a minor or catalyzing role) really lies.

## *Avoiding Over-Reaction*

Hence, the best advice one can give to democratic governments on international terrorism is not to over-react against this particular menace[7] and to attend to the vital strategic tasks of ensuring economic and political survival. There are of course, some useful practical steps that can be taken, for example among the EEC members, to improve the machinery of international police and security cooperation. Some of the more cost-effective of these possible measures are summarised below, and in the writer's view they would be worth adopting because they would help to save innocent lives and would substantially increase the rate of apprehension and conviction of terrorists. It would, moreover, be a great advantage if other states less advanced than Western Europe and the United States in their measures for international cooperation in this field could be encouraged to follow the West's example and to accede to, and implement, the basic international conventions and agreements designed to curb terrorism.

What is needed is a cool appraisal of the longer-term threat posed to liberal democratic society by terrorism, and the kind of measures that will help effectively to protect innocent life without sacrificing the rights of the individual. More radical responses involving sweeping emergency legislation and modification of normal judicial procedures and processes are not normally justified in the democratic West. The only exceptions are perhaps Northern Ireland and the Basque region in Spain where emergency powers have become necessary as a result of the worst protracted terrorist campaigns experienced in Western Europe in this century.

In the West such emergency or special powers would normally not only be unjustified and unnecessary; they would be totally counterproductive. For the real danger of resorting to sledge-hammer methods to cope with the relatively low intensities of political violence experienced in most Western countries is that they would extinguish democracy in the name of security. If we were to do this we would effectively be doing the terrorists' work for them and, moreover, with a speed and certainty that they themselves are incapable of achieving.

## Some Practical Steps

There are some valuable general measures, both national and international, that should be taken by the Western democracies. The steps summarised below would not be expensive to implement, and none of them could court the dangers of unbalanced response or over-reaction that have already been emphasized.

1. The Western democracies should patiently continue their efforts to alter the climate of international opinion to improve the long-term chances of creating a more effective framework of international law to deal with terrorism. Thus, despite all the difficulties and obstacles discussed earlier, all Western states should lend their diplomatic support, votes, and influence, in international organizations and conferences:

> To persuade nonratifying states to accede to existing useful multilateral agreements, such as the Tokyo, Hague and Montreal conventions to curb hijacking, to press for strengthening existing conventions, particularly in regard to enforcement provisions and sanctions, and
> To lend their full weight to useful fresh initiatives for international conventions. Even when it seems unlikely that a new initiative will surmount all the hurdles of international opposition, or when it is clear that only a handful of states will accord such measures immediate ratification, support is still worthwhile: if nothing else, it serves to educate the international community in the danger of terrorism and the vital need for international cooperation to counter it. Moreover, by exposing the opposition and obstruction of other states, such exercises help to identify the crypto-terrorist regimes. There is, furthermore, always the chance that the sheer weight of international pressure may cause a government to reconsider its earlier support for terrorism, or to move from neutrality or

ambivalence to positive support for humanitarian international measures designed to protect the innocent.

2. A second useful step would be to press for speedy ratification and implementation of the Council of Europe Convention on the Suppression of Terrorism, and the parallel European Community agreement.

3. A central coordinating antiterrorist cell of say half-a-dozen top security and intelligence experts, under the aegis of the EEC and with adequate research and administrative support and access to all meetings of Community Ministers of the Interior and Justice, and the intelligence and police chiefs of member states, could add immeasurably to the precision and quality of the international response. The new unit should provide expert analyses of intelligence data, assessment of capabilities and threats, a continuing research and development backup, including work on the pooling of counterterrorist weaponry and technology, training, joint exercises in hostage rescue, and advice to ministers and security services.

4. All democratic governments must hold firm to a strict policy of ''no deals with terrorists,'' and no submission to blackmail. Consistent national policies of minimizing terrorists' chances of rewards and maximizing the probability of punishment are most likely to stem the flow of terrorist killings in the longer term.

5. The democracies must also learn to defeat the terrorists' sustained propaganda war. Efforts to disguise themselves as legitimate ''freedom fighters'' must be exposed. The free media in particular owe a responsibility to the democratic societies which enable them to exist.[8] It is their job to expose the savage barbarism of the crimes and atrocities committed by terrorists. It is not their job to condone such acts or to lend murderers the freedom of the air to preach and promote more deaths. But, of course, in the last resort it is not a democracy's government or its security forces, or even its media that will determine the outcome of the long, long war against international terrorism: it is the degree of public support for democracy.

6. There is furthermore a real need for a voluntary and totally independent international organization to minister to the special needs of victims of international terrorism. Some governments, such as the Dutch in the wake of the South Moluccan attacks, have shown considerable imagination and insight in ministering to the needs of the survivors of terrorist incidents, and the families of the bereaved. The United Kingdom has

taken steps to provide for compensatory payments to victims of terrorist troubles, and for damage to property and business premises. By comparison with some of the awards, the pensions and other benefits for members of the security forces seem pitifully inadequate, and this is a matter the British government should attend to as a matter of urgency.

However, one must remember that in most countries victims of terrorism receive no assistance whatever from the state. And even where some provision exists there is often a vital need for medical and specialist services which only a voluntary organization could provide. Over most of the world these are forgotten people. Yet they often have the most desperate needs for specialist medical care, psychiatric help, and family and financial support. The proposed organization might perhaps be best established under the aegis of the International Red Cross. And of course, even if it proves necessary to set up a separate body, the advice and expertise of that body of mercy should be sought.

7. Finally, and once more taking into account the global context of modern international terrorism, I advocate the formation of special hostage-rescue commando units for every major region of the world. Such specialized units would be provided at the request of a government experiencing grave problems in coping with an international terrorist incident. They would be able to bring to bear on the situation all the latest techniques and technologies of siege management, hostage negotiation, and hostage rescue. It would be a valuable and positive step if the Council of Europe could make a start in proposing a standby unit of the kind for Europe. If this proves successful it could then provide a model for other regions of the world.

*Conclusions:* The most important consideration in arriving at an appropriate response to terror violence must be the strengthening of democracy and human rights. It is by these means above all that we can be sure of denying victory to those who have been corrupted by hatred and violence.

It is, of course, obvious that the judicial control of international response I have advocated is extremely difficult to apply rigorously, even in the confines of Western Europe. Special problems arise when lives of Western citizens are threatened by acts of terrorism undertaken with the full connivance and support of fanatical anti-Western regimes: e.g., Teheran. In such circumstances international law certainly permits a state to use limited force to rescue its endangered citizens. Military force must always be one option, but it must be remembered that such action may well threaten the lives not only of the hostages in the hands of the terrorists, but also the lives of large numbers of other innocent citizens. The chances of a successful Entebbe-style rescue operation must be weighed against the potentially wider dangers of armed intervention, and all possible diplomatic, moral, political, and economic pressures must be tried before resort to force.

## Notes

1. Frank Kitson, *Low Intensity Operations: Subversion, Insurgency and Peacekeeping* (London: Faber and Faber, 1971), p. 50.

2. Police used these qualities with notable success at the end of 1975 in their handling of the kidnapping of Dr. Tiede Herrema, a Dutch industrialist, in Eire, and of the Balcombe Street siege in London, which ended in the surrender of four IRA suspects. Many of the techniques of siege management used by the British police were pioneered by the New York Police Hostage Department.

3. Kitson, op. cit., Chap. 4, "The Army's Contribution," pp. 67 ff.

4. The only member states which refused to sign were Ireland and Malta.

5. Eighteen British soldiers were murdered in the Warrenpoint ambush on the same day that the Mountbatten boat was blown up at Mullaghmore.

6. This principle was strongly reiterated by the European Union of Police Federations at its conference in Cologne, September 19, 1979. The conference recommended the acceptance of a European police charter which includes the removal of political status from terrorist groups such as the IRA. It is noteworthy that this move was welcomed by the delegate from the Garda Police Association who stated, "The view of my association is that people who contravene the criminal code are only criminals and no cause can justify them being other than that."

7. One of the terrorists' major strategems is to provoke the authorities into a repressive over-reaction that will alienate the people and drive them into the arms of the terrorist movement. See Carlos Marighela, Minimanual of the Urban Guerrilla.

8. See *Television and Conflict*, ISC Special Report, May 1979.

# Index